THE SHEPHERD'S CHALLENGE

A CALL TO CHANGE THE CURRENT CHURCH CULTURE

ANDREW DELEE

xulon
PRESS

For Pastor Perry Keyt
My Pastor
My Mentor
My Friend

ACKNOWLEDGMENTS

First and foremost to Rhonda, my wife and soul mate. She has stood by me and helped carry the Heart of the Shepherd.

To my children Nathan, Kayla, Jennifer, Dana, Josh; and my grandchildren, Dax and Grayson, my most precious of sheep.

To the greatest church leadership a minister could ever have.

To Sarah, without whom I could not have written this book.

To Dana, for helping me focus.

To the greatest group of people on earth, the members of Voice to the Nations, to whom I pledge my life.

To Jesus, the Shepherd of my soul.

CONTENTS

FOREWORD

The Shepherd's Challenge is a must read for every pastor and church leader in America. It will challenge you as well as help equip you to recognize those who come into your churches disguised as shepherds when, in fact, they are not. Bishop Andrew DeLee is one of those rare leaders who has forged his way through many of life's challenges and has emerged victorious as a great Man of God with a true heart of a shepherd for the Body of Christ. His passion is to offer a challenging truth that this generation's pastors and leaders have overlooked. *Diligence* is doing a small thing for a long time until you get a big result. The True Shepherd Jesus Christ will never leave us or forsake us.

Imagine a church or a city that could have confidence that its pastor would never leave but was called to them for life because he was truly a shepherd after God's own heart. I once asked a retired pastor who had served in our city his whole life, "What do you think will be my biggest challenge as a young pastor desiring to change a city?" He stated, "Longevity!" Then he added, "When people used to come to a church, they stayed at that church; but this is not true with your generation." He said, "They will only be with you until they find something better or until hard times come along." Unfortunately, his words have proven true. So we have to ask ourselves the question, "Why?"

Genesis teaches us the principle that a seed reproduces after its own kind. Could it be that the reason why we see such a turnover in our church membership is that they've seen such turn over in us as pastors?

I know that God has a great plan for your life. I believe that God has put this book into your hands to take the shepherd's challenge: to understand the heart of a shepherd and the power of partnership. You can make a difference. As you open up your heart to the Holy Spirit, may everything that is inside you become a reality!

Sincerely,

Pastor Keith Ford

INTRODUCTION

I have a friend and leader in my church named John. When John was a teenager, he wanted to own the fastest car in town. He wanted a ride that was a real head turner. A car that not only was fast, but gorgeous as well. Then one day it came up for sale - the town hotrod. A Dodge Charger with a 455 Hemi. It was the envy of every teen in town. The shear sight of it sent testosterone flying. After saving his hard earned money, John went one afternoon and bought the car. He didn't take delivery of the car until the next day. As he began his victory lap through town to show everyone that he was now king of the hotrods, he realized something. The gentleman who sold him the car had switched the motors the night before John took possession. John was mad and frustrated, but he was unable to do anything about it because the car was sold "as is." He now owned a gorgeous car that couldn't outrun a Pinto. What a letdown! He expected to be able to rival the fastest of cars. He expected the chicks to fling themselves at him. Now he just had an ordinary car.

Sadly enough, this is what happens to people when they get saved and enter the Kingdom of God. They have expectations of coming into a body of believers that will believe in them and stick with them closer than their own brother. They dream of being able to outsmart or, at least, outrun the Devil with all his schemes. They think that their new church family is going to be there for them through thick and thin. After all, this is what they were told they were getting. But somewhere in the night, the ideals they heard were switched. Somewhere the promises of love, acceptance, and forgiveness were replaced with gossip, rejection, and gift tampering.

So as people enter the church, they either bail out because it's not what they thought, or they give into the insanity of the current Church culture. A culture that, despite popular opinion, is way too relevant to the world. It is one thing to be relevant in our dress, lingo, or music in order to win some to Christ, but we are being much too relevant in areas we shouldn't. Unfortunately, we look so much like the world that people see no difference so why should they bother with it all. Think about it. Our divorce rate is the same. The world and the Church have both been subject to the same types of scandals. We may look and talk differently, but our values seem to be way too similar.

It is not my desire to write another book on how awful the Church is. On the contrary, I believe that the Church is the answer for the crises we face on a daily basis. A unified Church can fix poverty, end world hunger, unify cultures, and bring sanity to politics. There's the clincher: a *unified* Church. It's crazy how many churches we have and still can't outrun the world in its attempt to win the favor of the human race. Why? It is my desire within the pages of this book to answer that question. I'm not so arrogant to think I have all the answers. But I do believe that I have been given a truth that can change the way not only the world views the Church, but also the way the Church views each other. We want to save the world; let's start with saving each other. Let's reach across the aisle and touch the life of the person sitting next to us. Before the church can show the world how much we love them, we have to be able to show each other.

"Therefore, as we have opportunity, let us do good to all people, especially to those who belong to the family of believers." - Galatians 6:10

God is calling the Church to do good to all people, but especially those who belong to the family of God. We must show the love for each other that Jesus showed to us. Then the world will know what they are buying.

Jesus was the good Shepherd. Aren't we supposed to be like Christ? This means we should be shepherding God's people like He did. I'm not just talking to pastors; I'm talking to the Body as a whole. Can we truly love like Jesus loved? Jesus demonstrated what it meant to have a shepherd's heart. He showed unconditional love for us. Think of it this way, Jesus died for you on your worst day.

That's right! Jesus went to the most depraved moment of your life and said, "I'll die for that moment." That's the heart of a shepherd.

Do you have the heart of a shepherd? Do you love people like Christ loved people? This book is your challenge; it's your moment to discover the real heart that is within you. So if you have the courage to find out what is really in you, read on.

1

SHEPHERD VS. HIRED HAND

We know the importance of unity when it comes to the Kingdom of God. In John 17:23, Jesus prays to the Father, *"May they be brought to complete unity to let the world know that you sent me and have loved them even as you have loved me."* The entire Bible reflects the theme of unity, and God desires His people to live in a place of true unity. This unity visibly displays what the power of God's love can accomplish in ordinary people. The church, of all places, should be where people genuinely love and care for one another. This is why the concept of partnership must be deposited into the hearts of God's people. This is why God desires to put in each of us the Shepherd's Heart.

"I am the good shepherd. The good shepherd lays down his life for the sheep." - John 10:11

Here Jesus declares, "I am the good Shepherd; the good Shepherd lays down his life for the sheep." A true shepherd's heart actually cares about the person sitting in the next pew, it actually prays for the guy running the soundboard, and it actually defends the worship leader when others are complaining about the music being too loud or too soft. Those who have the same heart as Jesus have a deep-seated love and concern for their brothers and sisters in the gospel and will even lay down their lives for one another.

God is calling his entire body to have the Shepherd's Heart, not just the pastor of a church. This is the type of love or partnership that God has destined us for, but how many churches are actually experiencing it? Many churches today are not filled with shepherds at all; they are filled with hired hands.

"The hired hand is not the shepherd who owns the sheep. So when he sees the wolf coming, he abandons the sheep and runs away. Then the wolf attacks the flock and scatters it. The man runs away because he is a hired hand and cares nothing for the sheep." - John 10:12-13

How could a hired hand abandon the sheep? He has the same skills as the shepherd; he carries the same kind of staff and slings the same kind of slingshot. So why run away? I'll tell you why. A hired hand has nothing invested. If there is no investment, why would the hired hand try to save the sheep? He has nothing to gain or lose.

That's why I believe that understanding the Shepherd's Heart is understanding ownership. Now I know we don't own each other in the literal sense, but in the spiritual sense we do. Ownership is when someone means so much to you that his/her loss would cause you pain.

> **A hired hand has nothing invested. If there is no investment why would the hired hand try to save the sheep? He has nothing to gain or lose.**

Unfortunately, that is not the attitude of a good portion of the Church. Far too often the Church echoes the same chant as the world does, "Your loss is my gain." When you've invested in a relationship, it is a lot harder to just walk away from that relationship. When you've spent time in prayer together, labored together, and shared the Word together, it is much harder to give up on that relationship even when you hit hard times. When you own something, that thing has value. When we have ownership in each other, we give greater value to one another.

If I walked out and someone had scratched my car, I would be upset. At the same time we see someone else's car get scratched and may feel bad, but ultimately we wouldn't care. If you were part owner in the car, then you would be equally upset. If two people have ownership in a relationship and the enemy tries to scratch it, they will both fight to make it right again.

It works the same way when you see hurting people. If you don't know the person, at best you may feel bad for them but you won't lose any sleep over it. If they are connected, partnered, and in your heart, you will suffer a loss.

Having someone in your heart means it will require some investing on your part. The reason you got upset about someone scratching your car is because it cost you something. In order to have relationships that go beyond the surface, you will have to invest in people's lives. Let's look at ways we invest.

YOU INVEST EVERY TIME YOU DEFEND THEIR HEART WHEN YOU CAN'T DEFEND THEIR ACTIONS.

It's easy to defend people who are always right, but what about the time they are visibly wrong and you're faced with the daunting challenge of defending their character even when you don't agree with their actions?

This is opportunity time. Are you going to invest, or are you going to join everybody else in the gossip fest? Are you going to add to the problem, or are you going to become part of the solution?

You've seen their character, and you know that what they did was an honest mistake; do you defend? Destiny will be tied to the saint who has the courage to stand up and say, "Stop! I know this person's character." Once gossip begins, relationship comes to an end. When you begin to speak and/or listen to gossip, you lose your connection to everything of value that person brings to you. You open yourself up to a world of suspicion that is very hard to recover from.

Let me take the gossip thought a little deeper if I may. Gossip takes on many forms. It's not just the blatant talking behind someone's back, but it is the deposit of suspicion as well. If in a conversation you place suspicion in my mind about someone, then you've gossiped. Have you heard it said, "It isn't gossip if it's true"? Yes, it is! Just because you are privy to the facts does not give you the right to share them.

Throughout this book you will often hear me refer to gossip. I hate gossip. God hates gossip. It is the black spot in the Church, the sin that counteracts God's purpose. When you defend, you walk in anti-gossip. It's just as easy to defend as it is to gossip.

Years ago I made a huge mistake as a youth pastor. We had a ski trip go very badly. It was totally my fault. I made mistake after mistake, and it ended in disaster. If you allow your mind to wonder about how badly a trip could go, mine was worse. To make matters worse, I didn't even know it went so wrong until I got home. Somehow, everyone on the trip kept me in the dark about all that happened right up until the moment I got off the bus. Upon arriving home, I was met with angry parents and an angry pastor. You should have seen the surprised look on my face when I arrived to see those angry people.

Although I had taken the youth group from eight to fifty in just a year and had seen great revival in the lives of the teens, I was faced with an unmerciful gauntlet of rage. No one defended me; no one defended my character. My pastor didn't defend me; none of the parents defended me. As a matter of fact, my pastor got on the phone and started calling other pastors telling them about it. I was getting phone calls from other youth pastors offering their condolences. I was humiliated and embarrassed.

I repented of my HONEST mistakes, but to no avail. I felt like I was being stoned. The teens responded to the gossip of the adults, and very quickly I lost their hearts as well. Only a couple of my youth workers stood up for me, but it wasn't enough. In the end I felt abandoned and worthless.

What would have happened if my pastor and the parents would have come to my rescue instead of kicking me while I was down? Many of the teens not only left the youth group, but they also left the church and, ultimately, God.

Don't get me wrong, I know this is difficult. We need to be careful whom we defend. If someone's previous character is not one to be desired then it's hard to

> **In a case where you can't defend, don't make matters worse by joining the assault.**

defend. But in a case where you can't defend, don't make matters worse by joining the assault. This is why partnership is so important; it allows you to see someone's character before the need to defend arises.

You invest every time you cry out to God on someone's behalf.

This is where true relationship starts. When you begin to pray for someone, something inside you shifts and you can't look at him/her the same way. The investment of your heart and God's presence does something inside of you. When your relationship with God is intertwined with a natural relationship, connection is made. That connection sets in motion a relationship that can't be easily broken.

"Though one may be overpowered, two can defend themselves. A cord of three strands is not quickly broken." - Ecclesiastes 4:12

When you pray for someone, you are becoming a cord of three. Your heart connects with God's Spirit, and God's Spirit connects with the person that you're interceding for. I truly believe that you can't cry and weep over someone's life without a connection being made. Why do you think Jesus tells us to pray for our enemies? You can't despise those you pray for.

Listen to Paul's voice as he writes these words:

"I thank God, whom I serve, as my forefathers did, with a clear conscience, as night and day I constantly remember you in my prayers. Recalling your tears, I long to see you, so that I may be filled with joy." - 2 Timothy 1:3-4

"God, whom I serve with my whole heart in preaching the gospel of his Son, is my witness how constantly I remember you in my prayers at all times; and I pray that now at last by God's will the way may be opened for me to come to you."
- Romans 1:9-10

"I thank my God every time I remember you. In all my prayers for all of you, I always pray with joy because of your partnership in the gospel from the first day until now."
- Philippians 1:3-5

Ponder on 2 Tim. 1:3-4. Paul is saying, "While I remember you in prayer, I recall my relational experiences I had with you." The bond between Paul and Timothy was strengthened by prayer. Paul took it so deep as to say, "That I may be filled with joy." Prayer brings joy to a relationship.

Have you ever prayed for someone to receive something special from God and then a few days or weeks later you see him walk in it? Experiences like that cause you to overflow with joy.

I have a friend who pastors a church in Florida. His name is Roger. This man is responsible for winning me to the Lord. This, by the way, was no small task. After I was saved, a bond was created between us that was awesome.

Now we live hundreds of miles apart and only get to see each other a couple of times a year as we both are responsible for great works of ministry. When we do get to see each other, it's like we've been together every day. How is this possible? When I pray for him, the joy of the relationship comes to the forefront of my heart. No matter how far away he may be, our relationship stays strong because we invest, through prayer, in each other.

YOU INVEST EVERY TIME YOU SHARE A WORD OF ENCOURAGEMENT.

Too often we don't realize the power of encouragement. We know the Word declares:

"The tongue has the power of life and death."
- Proverbs 18:21

If the tongue has power, that means our words have power.

When we encourage, we are releasing power into someone's life. When you take the time to speak into someone or write a note, you're investing into that person's future. You are giving value to someone's life.

Once you've given value to someone, it's not so easy to turn from that relationship. How long do we in the Church go without hearing a word of encouragement? I submit that it's probably about the same length of time we go without giving a word of encouragement.

Listen to what the writer of Hebrews says:

"But encourage one another daily, as long as it is called Today, so that none of you may be hardened by sin's deceitfulness." - Hebrews 3:13

Without daily encouragement, we are hardened by sin.

This is why so many in the Church are falling short of what God has for them. When the people of God begin to invest words of encouragement into one another, I believe churches will grow at a New Testament rate because people are getting grounded in their relationships.

Think about it, it's hard to get mad at someone who just told you he believes in you. My pastor used to tell me how much he believed in me. He would tell me I was going to do great things for the Kingdom of God, and I would one day do greater things than he did. He would also rake me over the coals if I got out of line. When I made a mistake, he held me accountable for that mistake, and sometimes it was not pleasant.

I remember sitting in front of his desk and his telling me to do something that I did not think I had time to do. I told him, "I'm stretched to the max." He replied, "You're not broke yet so get busy."

I could have gotten mad and left. I could have stormed out of his office, complained to everyone, and said this is too much. I could have quit, but I was stopped by a powerful force: his words of encouragement. Because he invested words of encouragement in me, I couldn't stay mad; I couldn't storm off. He could correct me without fear because he had invested his words of encouragement in me.

To this day, even after his passing, he still encourages me. I have a book that contains all the letters of encouragement that he ever wrote me. When I need to be lifted up and there is no one around, I go to my letters. After reading them, I feel like I can again walk out my destiny.

> **Woe to the Shepherd who tries to correct without first investing words of encouragement.**

Woe to the Shepherd who tries to correct without first investing words of encouragement.

2

THE THREE PLAYERS

There are essentially three players within the church.

"I am the good shepherd. The good shepherd lays down his life for the sheep. The hired hand is not the shepherd who owns the sheep. So when he sees the wolf coming, he abandons the sheep and runs away. Then the wolf attacks the flock and scatters it. The man runs away because he is a hired hand and cares nothing for the sheep." - John 10:11-13

WOLF

Let's not kid ourselves; we know who this joker is. He's called by many names in the Word of God. We call him Lucifer, Serpent, Deceiver, and, of course, the Devil. We know he comes to steal, to kill, and to destroy.

"Therefore Jesus said again, 'I tell you the truth, I am the gate for the sheep. All who ever came before me were thieves and robbers, but the sheep did not listen to them. I am the

gate; whoever enters through me will be saved. He will come in and go out, and find pasture. The thief comes only to steal and kill and destroy; I have come that they may have life, and have it to the full.'" - John 10:7-10

Jesus offers safety to the sheep, but the thief comes to steal, kill, and destroy. Make no mistake. There is an enemy, a wolf, trying to corrupt the sheep. It's not a matter of *if* the enemy of our soul will attack, it's a matter of *when* he will attack.

Notice the wolf's primary focus: to scatter the flock. I wish the church would truly grasp this. Every attack on our church and all our petty differences is for one purpose: to scatter

> **Every attack on our church and all our petty differences is for one purpose: to scatter us.**

us. The enemy knows if we are scattered we are ineffective. Only the unified Church can accomplish great things for the Kingdom of God.

How many churches that are full of disunity actually grow? If we know that every attack is to bring disunity, why do we fall so easily to the devil's schemes? I'll say this: a person with a true Shepherd's heart can't fall to them, only a hired hand can. Believe me, that's why the enemy doesn't want you to get a hold of the Shepherd's heart. What can the devil do with a church full of people who have a heart like that of the great Shepherd? It is one thing for the Devil to duck when the shepherd behind the pulpit swings his rod, but it's another thing for the Devil to duck when the whole house of shepherds are swinging their rods.

Don't be deceived, not every wolf is the devil himself. There are wolves in the church that are sent there by the devil. They may not look like the devil, but you can always spot them. They're the people who come in with their own agenda, their own vision to try and steal the sheep for their own purpose. They're not for the church, but they need the church to accomplish the work of the enemy.

Often times they don't even realize they are being used by the enemy. But we've all seen it. A wolf comes to the church, steals a few sheep, then goes to the other side of town, starts another church, and calls it *breakthrough*. Six months later, that church busts up and the sheep are left scattered and disillusioned. Sadly, many will never darken the doors of a church again.

I had a heartbreaking conversation with a man who used to come to our church. He had left when a group of people followed a wolf to go start another church. After a couple of months at their new church home, they began to see a heart of a wolf and not the heart of a shepherd. They left the church, but went nowhere else. A year later, the wife of the couple left the husband for another woman, leaving the family shattered, and a husband broken and depressed.

On one occasion a homeless man came into our church and convinced one of our members that we were not of God because we didn't sell all we had and give to the poor. This man took his family that was very active in worship and the youth ministry out of the church. A few weeks later the homeless man was gone, but it was too late. The wife left, and the husband called me in tears wanting to know if all was lost because he had allowed a wolf to pull him away.

The Word tells us of the fate of those who do such things. Jeremiah 23:1 says, *"Woe to the shepherds who are destroying and scattering the sheep of my pasture!"* I believe a harsh judgment is coming on these wolves in shepherd's clothing.

HIRED HAND

We didn't need to spend much time on the wolves, since we know who they are, but let us dig a little deeper into the hired hand.

I first ask myself the question, why would someone be a hired hand when there is opportunity to be a shepherd? It's like asking someone if they want to work for a company or own a company. So let's look at it from that aspect. Why would someone want to work for a company instead of own it?

Maybe laziness? It takes less effort to punch a clock than it does to run the company. How many people that punch a clock take the work home with them? Not many. In the Kingdom of God, we have Christians who punch a spiritual clock. They punch in on Sunday and punch out at 12:00pm on the dot. They don't think about the flock again until next Sunday. Some may say that's the pastor's job.

Hold on. Remember, we are believing God for all the saints of God to become shepherds of each other. Relationships with other sheep take work, and lazy hired hands don't like to work. Sometimes you have to work hard at liking people, because not all people are easy to like.

Now let's be honest, there are times when God sends us people that are not our cup of tea. Sometimes we meet people whose inward character is hidden by an outward struggle. We can't be lazy and not dig past someone's surface, because surfaces don't always reveal someone's true potential. A hired hand will never take the time to dig deep enough to see someone's true character. A hired hand won't get out of his comfort zone to get to know someone better.

Think of how many times you've avoided people because their personality was different from yours. Then you were, for whatever reason, forced to get to know them

> **Sometimes we meet people whose inward character is hidden by an outward struggle.**

only to find out you had things in common, and they were not so bad after all. Once you know someone on a deeper level, it is impossible to be a hired hand, but we will deal with getting to know someone better in later chapters.

Have you ever noticed a hired hand will refrain from helping sheep? It is because he struggles to help himself. These are the ones that have not allowed the Good Shepherd to take care of them. It's hard to help take care of others if you're not taking care of yourself.

If you even try, your weakness will be exposed and no one likes his weakness exposed. No one wants to look like he doesn't have his act together. It's hard to help people when you yourself are a mess.

Often times when the wolf attacks and the hired hand runs away, it's because of pure selfishness. They are too worried about their own skin to worry about you. A fear hits them when they see you attacked, because they don't want to have to fight. A hired hand is like the warrior sitting in a recliner; they are too comfortable to go and fight. King David, in all his greatness, was considered the great shepherd of Israel, but there was a time when David slipped off into a hired hand mentality.

Examine this passage.

"In the spring, at the time when kings go off to war, David sent Joab out with the king's men and the whole Israelite army. They destroyed the Ammonites and besieged Rabbah. But David remained in Jerusalem." – 2 Samuel 11:1

David was at home being selfish when he was supposed to be at war for and with the sheep of Israel. He was thinking of himself when he was supposed to be thinking of others. This is a trait of a hired hand, thinking of himself when he should have been thinking of the sheep.

Not only will a hired hand not be there for the sheep, but also he himself will suffer a major fall. We see this in the life of David when he committed adultery and murder. All this happened because he was not fighting for the sheep when he was supposed to be.

A hired hand will always want to know what's in it for him. After all, a hired hand has no share in the inheritance, so he has to get something out of the deal.

Only the shepherd has access to the inheritance left to him by the one who owns the sheep. A hired hand merely gets a salary. How many people have we seen in the Church who only receive a salary from God, when they could be getting an inheritance? You see being a hired hand means having to forfeit your rights to an inheritance. A hired hand's ambition will be to succeed at the cost of the sheep, not for the cause of the sheep.

When it's all broken down, the hired hand runs because he simply doesn't love the sheep. He loves only himself. When you love something, you can't abandon it in its darkest hour. When you love something, you can't sit by and watch it be destroyed. At Voice to the Nations, we don't sit by and watch as our brothers and sisters are eaten. We get out our staffs and start beating the enemy. What kind of person can see a fallen brother and add to his pain by gossiping or by kicking?

> **What kind of person can see a fallen brother and add to his pain by gossiping or by kicking?**

Don't think you can ride the fence either. You can't love them today while things are great for them and then kick them tomorrow while they're down. Hired hands better fear the judgment that is coming on them.

A hired hand will leave a church at the first sign of trouble. Trouble meaning he didn't get his way or he was bitten by another sheep.

The hired hand will leave the first time his comfort zone is violated. The first time he no longer feels that he can remain at his current growth level, he will leave.

A hired hand can't handle being challenged. He thinks a challenge is an attack against him personally; in reality, a challenge is just an opportunity to grow in the Kingdom of God. I wonder how much growth is lost on people who got offended when they got challenged?

Growth is a foreign concept to a hired hand. A hired hand can't grow, because that would mean he had to work, serve, walk in humility, and submit to an authority.

SHEPHERD

Shepherds are what God is calling His Church to become. I believe Jesus is longing for His Church to truly begin to shepherd one another. Jesus' central message was for us not just to get along, but also to serve one another.

Think of it this way. Do we call ourselves Christians? Do we proclaim to be Christ-like? If yes, then we have to model the heart of the Shepherd. We have to love like He loved, serve like He served, and forgive like He forgave. What would Jesus' response be to your getting mad because someone hurt your feelings? Would Jesus abandon the sheep because they didn't invite him to dinner? Could Jesus leave you because he didn't get to sing a special? How would Jesus react if you left because the pastor made you stand too long?

I don't know about you, but the whole concept of being a hired hand versus being the shepherd seems like a no brainer. Just look at the benefits and rewards. The benefits to being a shepherd far outweigh the benefits to being a hired hand. Observe these verses:

"And there were shepherds living out in the fields nearby, keeping watch over their flocks at night. An angel of the Lord appeared to them, and the glory of the Lord shone around them, and they were terrified. But the angel said to them, 'Do not be afraid. I bring you good news of great joy that will be for all the people. Today in the town of David a Savior has been born to you; he is Christ the Lord. This will be a sign to you: You will find a baby wrapped in cloths and lying in a manger.' Suddenly a great company of the heavenly host appeared with the angel, praising God and saying, 'Glory to God in the highest, and on earth peace to men on whom his favor rests.' When the angels had left them and gone into heaven, the shepherds said to one another, 'Let's go to Bethlehem and see this thing that has happened, which the

Lord has told us about.' So they hurried off and found Mary and Joseph, and the baby, who was lying in the manger. When they had seen him, they spread the word concerning what had been told them about this child, and all who heard it were amazed at what the shepherds said to them. But Mary treasured up all these things and pondered them in her heart. The shepherds returned, glorifying and praising God for all the things they had heard and seen, which were just as they had been told." – Luke 2:8-20

Here we read of the glorious birth of our Lord. Jesus has just been sent to earth to set mankind free, and who gets to see him first? Shepherds! Shepherds who were watching their flock at night. While darkness reigned, the shepherds were watching.

Isn't it awesome that God chose shepherds, who were busy looking after the flock, to be the first ones to hear about our Savior? The revelation of the coming of the Son of God was given to them. I believe this is true for us today. While we are watching after the flock of God, while we are being our brother's keeper, revelation is coming to us. If you need a fresh word from God, I suggest that you get busy looking after God's people. Only those who are watching out for God's sheep need a revelation from Him. If God gives you anything, it's going to be for the people that you serve with.

I've often heard people make the statement, "I need a word from the Lord." My question is what for? Why do you need God to speak to you? God speaks when our motives are pure and our agenda is about His sheep.

3

CHARACTERISTICS OF A SHEPHERD

I heard Prophet John Gray once say, "God is more worried about your character than He is the assignment that you're on." Wow! How true is that? God is more worried about the character of the shepherd than He is the act of shepherding.

The character of the shepherd is developed over time. That means you have to stay with the sheep long enough to allow your heart and life to mesh with theirs.

Let's observe some qualities that a shepherd must have.

A SHEPHERD LEADS BY EXAMPLE.

Listen to the boldness of Paul in these passages.

"Therefore I urge you to imitate me." – 1 Corinthians 4:16

"For you yourselves know how you ought to follow our example." – 2 Thessalonians 3:7

"Follow my example, as I follow the example of Christ." – 1 Corinthians 11:1

How many people in the Kingdom of God can say this? Paul is telling these churches, "If I do it; you can do it." A good shepherd will never go somewhere his sheep can't go. Some may say that they don't want people following them, but it doesn't matter who you are, someone is following you. Everyone is a shepherd to someone, whether you like it or not.

> **Follow me as I follow Christ. I wonder how many Christians have the nerve to say this.**

When my children were young, my wife and I told them that they could do whatever they saw us doing.

We made it clear that we were taking on the responsibility of being their example. This meant that for years we watched cartoons and kid's shows on television. I was ready to kill one purple dinosaur.

Even when the kids went to bed, we didn't watch anything that would affect them in a negative way. Our children never even thought about smoking or drinking while they were growing up, because they didn't see us doing it.

I remember when my son started to drive, which is scary for any parent. As he got behind the wheel of the car and started down the road, he began to go a few miles over the speed limit. His mother told him to keep it at the speed limit. His response was, "Dad goes a few miles over the speed limit." Oops! He was following my example.

So here is the question we all need to ask ourselves. Is there anything in our lives that would lead the sheep astray? A true shepherd's desire is to see the sheep go in the right direction. That may mean having to give up something that would harm a lamb. What about the words that come out of your mouth? Can they be repeated? What if your son or daughter repeated a joke you told? Would it be acceptable? Would you be embarrassed if your son or daughter quoted your conversation about the pastor? What about your phone conversation with Mrs. I-gotta-know?

Here's a challenge for you. Can you be repeated? Can what you say be shouted from the rooftops without consequences?

Notice again what Paul said, *"Follow my example, as I follow the example of Christ"*. This means we need to be following Christ as closely as we can. If we are to be shepherds, we need to know every move the Good Shepherd makes.

Listen to the words of Jesus in John 10:14, *"I am the good shepherd; I know my sheep and **my sheep know me.**"* Do you know Jesus enough to represent him? Are you ambassador material? That's what Jesus is looking for: shepherds who, with boldness, can represent him. He's looking for shepherds who can look at the masses and with boldness declare like Paul, "Follow me because I'm following the Good Shepherd."

This means that hypocrisy can no longer exist. People are looking for leaders that are real, not plastic. I hear the cry of the world saying, "Give us someone to follow that we can trust." They're looking for shepherds who are not feeding them with one hand while hiding something with the other.

A SHEPHERD STANDS WATCH OVER THE FLOCK.

Can you hear the words of Jeremiah?

"Hear the word of the LORD, O nations; proclaim it in distant coastlands: 'He who scattered Israel will gather them and will watch over his flock like a shepherd.'" – Jeremiah 31:10

In order to understand this you have to look at the lifestyle of a shepherd. A shepherd was so concerned over his sheep that he rarely slept at night. As a matter of fact, sleep to a shepherd is a luxury that most don't get. A shepherd is ever watching to make sure that no wolf comes anywhere near his sheep.

"Be self-controlled and alert. Your enemy the devil prowls around like a roaring lion looking for someone to devour." – 1 Peter 5:8

A wolf will lurk all around the camp at night, but he's not watching the sheep. He's watching the shepherd. If the shepherd falls asleep, he can attack without fear of being detected. How many weak Christians are picked off because a shepherd was not watching out for them?

Some would say, "But I'm weak. I can't look after the flock tonight." Jesus addresses this point.

> **A wolf will lurk all around the camp at night, but he's not watching the sheep. He's watching the shepherd.**

"Then he said to them, 'My soul is overwhelmed with sorrow to the point of death. Stay here and keep watch with me.' Then he returned to his disciples and found them sleeping. 'Could you men not keep watch with me for one hour?' he asked Peter. 'Watch and pray so that you will not fall into temptation. The spirit is willing, but the body is weak.'" - Matthew 26:38-41

Jesus was saying, "I know you're weak, but this is important." Your weakness should not stand in the way of your watching out for the flock of God.

I remember one Sunday I came to church and just before I went out to preach I started getting sick. Leaders around me were standing ready to go in my stead, but I knew in my heart that I had the word for the sheep. I went to the bathroom, got sick, went out there and preached the message God had put on my heart. The altars filled with people needing prayer, and I was getting sicker. I managed to pray for the people; but after I was finished, I was finished. My wife took me home where I collapsed in my bed. I could have went home and left it up to my leaders (and they would have done a fine job, I might add), but I was the one to watch over the sheep that day. Many people were set free because I was willing to watch when I was weak.

I think of my precious pastor. He was suffering from lung cancer and week after week he kept getting in the pulpit and preaching to the flock God had put in his charge. He never wavered in his calling to the sheep he so dearly loved. Until the end, he thought of them.

And then there was Arnold, my uncle and a faithful member of my church. He was dying of cancer and was confined to a wheel-chair. Despite this, Sunday after Sunday he was in the house worshipping and being an example of faithfulness. Nobody missed church in those days. They would say, "If Arnold is there, then how could I miss?"

How often have we used the excuse that we are having a hard time to stop us from being there for our brothers and keeping watch over them? Being hard pressed is no excuse for not watching over your brother.

"We are hard pressed on every side, but not crushed; perplexed, but not in despair; persecuted, but not abandoned;

struck down, but not destroyed. We always carry around in our body the death of Jesus, so that the life of Jesus may also be revealed in our body." – 2 Corinthians 4:8-10

Too often we focus on the pressed, perplexed, persecuted, and the struck down, but Paul says don't look at that. Look at the fact that you're not crushed, not in despair, not abandoned, and not destroyed. If we focus on the latter, then we will be able to watch over our brothers at all times.

We can't talk about watching over our brothers without talking about the convenience factor, or shall I say the inconvenience factor? We are willing to be there for our brothers as long as it is convenient. The moment we are put out, well, that's a different story.

Have you ever seen someone have a problem or tragedy at a convenient time? No one has ever died in my church when I had some down time. The call from the hospital always comes during dinner. A baby is always born at 2:00 a.m. That couple is always going to want to get married at the same time I planned my vacation.

Being there for sheep is not about convenience; it's about sacrifice. This same principle has to flow over into the pews.

I am so proud of how my church responds to someone's death. It's as if that family is the most important family on the planet. The flock comes together and responds to the needs of the family in a big way. So big even the local funeral director likes it when our church is involved in the process.

The sheep-shepherd has to rise up and say, "I'll watch over my brother." Think what kind of revival will break out if we start watching over one another with the love of the Good Shepherd.

A SHEPHERD PROTECTS THE SHEEP FROM THE ELEMENTS.

We can hear it off in the distance, thunder cracking loud applause. But the applause is not for us, nor is it a good thing. A storm is coming. I can imagine a shepherd standing with his flock and hearing that sound. He probably takes a deep breath and realizes it's time to go to work protecting the sheep from the weather. You see, in times of bad weather a shepherd has to step it up a notch.

He may have been just going along doing the routine, but now he has to go to work. I see the same thing in the Church. Shepherds are going along and everything seems to be fine until all of a sudden a storm hits and sheep start panicking. Sometimes there is no shelter to run to; sometimes we have to weather the storms of life.

As a shepherd, what do you do? Do you rally your courage and help the other sheep, or do you add to the chaos?

Too often we think when someone hits a storm in life that it's his own fault, and a lot of times it is. But whether it's his fault or not, we shouldn't abandon the sheep when they're faced with bad weather. That would make us fair weather shepherds, wouldn't it? You want to be there and help as long as it's easy and not demanding.

What about the times when a sheep makes a demand on your heart that you were not prepared for? They're facing a storm that you've never faced, a trial that you've never encountered. Do you panic and run? A true shepherd realizes that you don't have to have all of life's answers to be there for someone. Sometimes providing shelter means just being a shoulder to cry on or an ear to listen.

We as a Church tend to hide behind our inadequacies when it comes to other people's inadequacies. I know, as a pastor, I have faced this problem many times. You know, the "I don't have the answer" problem. It does not mean that I abandon the sheep. I tell them I don't have the answer, and we work through the storm together.

I wonder how many sheep have left the fold because there was no one there for them. They hit a storm and because of previous experiences they bail out instead of seeking help from the other sheep. They've been let down too many times.

At my church we have worked hard to create an atmosphere that allows people who make a mistake or hit a storm to seek help. If hurting people are confident that others are not going to add to their wounds, they are more likely to seek help.

The generation that we are living in is putting a greater demand on the shepherds of the house. A couple of generations ago, all you needed to do was be there for people when their love one passed away, provide food for the family and a shoulder to cry on. Maybe help out a single mom. But now it's a whole new world. We have to deal with members on pain pills, half the congregation divorcing, affairs in the church, clashes of band members, child molesters, and every other sin you can think of.

> **The generation that we are living in is putting a greater demand on the shepherds of the house.**

There is a greater demand on the shepherd, and that's why God is trying to raise up people who will carry his heart to the hurting person sitting in the pew with them. You don't have to have the answers, just the heart of the shepherd. Jesus wouldn't write people off, so why do we?

Here's what I've found: people tend to add to the storm instead of provide shelter from the storm. The Church is notorious for taking a thunderstorm and making it a tornado. I know we've heard it before, but the Church tends to kick people while they are down. Instead of ministering to a couple that's struggling, we gossip about them. Instead of helping a single mom, we judge her. Someone in the church falls, and it's the church member who calls the media just so he can get his name in the paper. A minister falls, and we never even consider praying for him. We get in our corners and begin telling people that we knew something was not right.

Be ever so careful when it comes to the shepherds who stand behind the pulpits of this generation. They are God's anointed, and the Bible is clear on touching God's anointed. 1 Chronicles 16:22 tells us, *"Do not touch my anointed ones; do my prophets no harm."* It's not our responsibility to judge those who God anoints; God will judge them. The church creates its own havoc. We make the devil's job easy. A true shepherd loves and covers. Notice I didn't say cover up. It's our job to cover with love, and it is God's job to expose whom he wants. Let's let God do his job, and let us do ours.

A SHEPHERD IS ABLE TO FIGHT FOR HIS SHEEP.

There is a point I want to bring out here. It's not whether you're willing to fight, it's are you able to fight? Notice the disciples here.

"Watch and pray so that you will not fall into temptation. The spirit is willing, but the body is weak." – Matthew 26:41

They were willing but were not able. The disciples wanted to be there for Jesus but simply couldn't. Too often in the church we are willing to do something for other sheep, but we are not able. We talk about going into battle for our brothers, but are we able to fight? Watch the great shepherd David.

"Your servant has killed both the lion and the bear; this uncircumcised Philistine will be like one of them, because he has defied the armies of the living God. The LORD who delivered me from the paw of the lion and the paw of the

bear will deliver me from the hand of this Philistine." – 1
Samuel 17:36-37

It was the lion and the bear that enabled David to defeat Goliath. You will never defeat other people's Goliath until you've defeated your own lion and bear.

It is hard to tell someone to get off drugs while you're still using drugs. It's hard to pray for someone's marriage when your marriage is a wreck. If you don't have a prayer life and your brother needs you to pray for him, you're not going to all of a sudden get a prayer life. If someone needs a word from the Lord, what are you going to do? Blow the dust off your Bible and give him one? You have to already be praying; the word needs to be already in you.

> **If someone needs a word from the Lord what are you going to do? Blow the dust off your Bible and give him one?**

Before I came to know the Lord I was a true heathen. Every year we would go to the NASCAR races. (This in no way is a condemnation of all the great NASCAR fans out there.) One year my brother and his best friend got into a fight. Now keep in mind, we were all inebriated to say the least. One of the guys we were partying with broke up the fight and proceeded to win my brother and his best friend to Jesus.

To my surprise, my brother and his best friend were crying and repenting. They, without shame, were having a moment with the Lord, right in the middle of the infield.

But here's the problem: the guy who shared Jesus with them was drunker than they were! I proceeded to share this fact with them. (Keep in mind, I was not yet saved.) They quickly realized that religion was not for them and went back to drinking.

What if a real shepherd had been there that night? He could have brought revival to NASCAR. My brother and his best friend could have had a genuine experience with God. Instead salvation for my brother was delayed fifteen years.

A SHEPHERD PROVIDES A SENSE OF PEACE FOR THE SHEEP.

To put it simply, if you have a freaked out shepherd, you'll have freaked out sheep. People are looking for a place to escape from their chaos.

People are facing chaos in their relationships and in their marriages. They are facing a lack of peace in their homes, and they come to the church to find a sense of peace.

What do the shepherds of the house offer? Let me share with you the importance of peace. Before I got saved, I was a bad drug addict. I used to go days without sleep. I remember finally giving in to the guy who was trying to win me to the Lord. We went to church that night, but I didn't get saved because I was afraid of going to hell, or because I wanted to go to heaven. I got saved because I wanted to go sleep in peace. I was searching for peace, and when I found it, it was like a great treasure that was hidden for years.

We discover peace from people who are carrying it and are willing to share it. I sometimes wonder what a visitor of a church thinks when he sees the house in chaos. When there is tension on the praise team, and tension in leadership, and tension among the shepherd/sheep, visitors know it, and their ability to get what they need from God is gone.

The Good Shepherd is the Prince of Peace. That means we should be walking not just *in* peace, but we also should be walking *out* peace. In other words, we should be living a life of peace. Our daily walk with the Lord should be filled with peace. People will recognize that peace and seek you out.

I have a colored past that was filled with drug and alcohol addiction. After I got saved and received the peace I needed, I - like a lot of addicts - relapsed and ended up in prison. Upon being released from prison, I went straight into rehab to get everything I needed to stay clean once I finally hit the streets. Every night I found myself in the chapel praying for God to keep me strong once I got home. And strength I found; not only strength but also added peace as well.

Remember people will recognize your peace and seek you out. As I began to get serious about my walk with God, there was a young man named Tim that just started coming to the rehab who kept watching me. He would stare at me and listen to everything I said. One night, as I was in the chapel praying, Tim tapped me on the shoulder. He asked me if he could have what I had, if he could have the peace that I had so obviously found. I told Tim about what the Lord had done for me, and how the Lord had saved me. That night I prayed with Tim, and he gave his heart to the Lord and found the peace that I had exhibited. A side note here. I came back years

> **Sheep/shepherds should be oozing the peace of God. The person in the pew next to you is looking for it.**

later to speak at that rehab, and Tim was the new director!

The sheep/shepherds should be oozing the peace of God. The person in the pew next to you is looking for it.

A SHEPHERD CARRIES THE WOUNDED.

If you study the life of shepherds, you will find that they have a special love for their sheep. Whenever a sheep in their flock got wounded by a wolf, or accident, they would pick up the sheep and carry it until it was able to walk on its own again.

Whenever the shepherd did this, it would cause a close relationship to be formed between the shepherd and the sheep. Wherever the shepherd went, the sheep would follow closely behind. If a case came up where all the sheep ran off, the wounded sheep would still stay by the shepherd's side. Thus, the wounded sheep became the shepherd's greatest asset. I wish the church would truly get this.

It's the wounded sheep that you picked up that remains the most loyal in times of trial. That person sitting next to you that has been struggling for the past year may need you to carry them awhile. You never know, they may become your most trusted friend.

But too often this is not what we do. We're afraid of getting too close to the sin to pick up the sinner. We look for God to send us perfect people, but all we get is wounded people. If they were perfect, they wouldn't need us, now would they?

> **It's the wounded sheep that you picked up that remain the most loyal in times of trial.**

Years ago my wife and I began ministering to a wounded sheep named Melanie. Melanie was struggling with addiction among other issues. She was not only an addict, but she was a dealer to boot. Well, this got her into a lot of trouble, and she wound up in jail. My wife and I began to visit her in jail. She was resistant at first but eventually realized that she needed to return to her place in the body of Christ. She got out of jail and became a committed disciple for Christ. She became so committed to the youth that she eventually became the full-time youth pastor at our church for a season. Since that time we've had to address other struggles with family and even a successful bout with cancer. Through it all, she has remained loyal to my wife and me and is still as committed, if not more committed, to the cause of Christ than ever before. My wife and I could not be more proud of the wife, mother, and minister that she has become.

Let's shift to a tougher area. If a sheep is prone to running off, the shepherd would have to do the unthinkable. He would take the sheep and break his leg so he would *have* to depend on the shepherd for everything.

This seems like a cruel thing to do on the surface, but in reality it's the most humane thing to do. If the sheep keeps running off, then how is the shepherd going to protect him?

What if we started doing this in the church? When sheep keep running off, we just break their legs so they have to be there. The next time a husband has an affair and wants to leave his wife – break a leg. The next time a teenager wants to try drugs – break a leg. The next time someone starts gossiping – cut out their tongue. Not sure if that would go over well. But I do believe it's time for the church to show some moxie and walk in tough love.

Look at what the Bible teach us in Galatians.

"Brothers, if someone is caught in a sin, you who are spiritual should restore him gently. But watch yourself, or you also may be tempted. Carry each other's burdens, and in this way you will fulfill the law of Christ." – Galatians 6:1-2

Did you hear what Paul said? Restore gently and then carry one another's burdens. We do the opposite. We curse harshly and drop people like they have the plague.

When was the last time you got over your holy self and carried someone through a season of struggle? Notice I said carry but don't condone. Help bear the burden but don't belittle the sin.

Here's a challenge for you. Do you look at other people's faults and judge? Or do you try to figure out a way to carry them through their temptation?

A SHEPHERD CARRIES THE NEWBORNS.

When a sheep is first born, it comes out wobbly-legged, confused, and disoriented. It is the shepherd's responsibility to carry the newborn while it's learning to walk.

If the shepherd did not carry the newborn, it would most likely not make it. This is where the shepherds of a house really have to shine. We have to start carrying the newborns.

We finally convince someone that Jesus is the way. We get him to come to an altar, confess his sins, and accept the gift of salvation. The next thing we do is walk away and hope they grow up to be a strong Christian just like us.

Are you kidding me? How is a newborn Christian going to be able to make it in this cruel world if there is no one there to guide him/her. They're headed into a field full of wolves and they don't even know it, much less how to deal with the enemy when he attacks.

I recently became a G-Pa (that's the coolest way I could think of to be called a grandfather). When my grandsons are in my care, I can't keep my eyes off them. I'm constantly worried that they are going to get into something that will harm them.

A true shepherd should feel that way about his sheep. Don't cop-out on me here. Remember we are all shepherds; some just sit in a pew. We should be looking after the newborns in the Kingdom like we look after the newborns in our lives.

We tend to be out of balance when it comes to new Christians. I see one of two things usually happening. Number one, we will expect the newborn Christian to do all the right things because, after all, we have a great church. When they don't, we just figure that salvation must not have sunk in, so we go on to the next person.

Secondly, we will see that new convert do *so* well that we will assume they are destined for greatness (which all Christians are), but we will thrust them immediately to the front of the room. But listen to Paul's warning concerning leaders in the church.

> **We expect the new born Christian to do all the right things, because, after all, we have a great church.**

"He must not be a recent convert, or he may become conceited and fall under the same judgment as the devil."
– 1 Timothy 3:6

We have to be careful, or we will be setting up that newborn Christian to fall into pride just like the Devil fell into pride.

Newborn Christian should be handled with care and love.

I got saved in an amazing time at my church. We were in a great revival. I got to go to church every night, and that kept me pretty fired up; but soon the revival ended, and I needed more. I began attending these Bible studies every week, and, man, they were great. We got deep teaching, and I grew a lot, but one instance could have driven me away forever if it had not been for some deep relationships I had.

One night during our Bible study, the teacher asked a question about the oil in the lamps of the ten virgins. I immediately spoke up, as I was prone to having a big mouth, and said I believed it represented the Holy Spirit. Not a bad answer for a three month old Christian, I thought. But the teacher began to rake me over the coals, telling me I assumed too much and went as far as saying he didn't like me. I was mortified. Luckily, there were friends there who consoled me, or I would have not only bailed on church but also may have jumped him (remember I wasn't saved long).

A true shepherd walks gently with the newborn sheep in the flock.

A SHEPHERD GUARDS HIMSELF FROM MONOTONY.

Let's be real: boredom is real in the Church. People get bored serving the Lord. Boredom usually becomes a problem because shepherds get tired of doing the same old thing.

Boredom will always lead to neglect. If we get bored with the sheep at church, we will neglect them. But the Bible is clear about what we are to do in this matter.

"Let us not become weary in doing good, for at the proper time we will reap a harvest if we do not give up. Therefore, as we have opportunity, let us do good to all people, especially to those who belong to the family of believers." – Galatians 6:9-10

There are three things I want you to observe in this passage. First, if we don't grow weary in well doing, we will reap a harvest. The harvest comes to the shepherds who don't give up on the sheep.

Secondly, we are to do good to all people. That's all sheep. Even the sheep you don't like right now. We don't have the authority to pick and choose whom we are going to get to minister to.

And thirdly, he said to especially do good to those who belong to the church. Let me go ahead and kill a sacred cow here. We are supposed to help those who belong to the Kingdom of God above those who are still in the world.

This is powerful, because we think we should always put the lost first. In reality, we are to put one another first. This is because if we have a happy, healthy body, then ministering to the lost is automatic. We have a misconception: we think we attract the world by giving to them, but in reality we attract the world by being there for each other. We are giving the world a reason to want to be a part of what we have when we care for one another.

The bottom line is this: boredom in the Church is nothing more than people becoming too familiar with their surroundings. Shepherds mess up when they become so familiar with the sheep God puts in their life that they take them for granted.

A SHEPHERD PASSES ALL THE SHEEP UNDER HIS ROD.

Every night the shepherd would gather the sheep so they could pass under his rod. This was done so the shepherd could count the sheep to make sure none were missing. This is when the verse in Matthew comes to life.

"What do you think? If a man owns a hundred sheep, and one of them wanders away, will he not leave the ninety-nine on the hills and go to look for the one

> **Every night the shepherd would gather the sheep so they could pass under his rod. This was done so the shepherd could count the sheep to make sure none were missing.**

that wandered off? And if he finds it, I tell you the truth, he is happier about that one sheep than about the ninety-nine that did not wander off." – Matthew 18:12-13

Why is he happier about the one sheep than the other ninety-nine? Because the ninety-nine are secure.

If you study the scripture, you will find that the Church is always compared to a woman or a wife. If you know anything about women, you will know that they need security. If the Church is offering security, then the sheep tend not to roam, but we will get to that later.

Look around your church. Do you see some that are missing? Are there sheep that have wandered off? If you do, it's your responsibility to go get them.

A SHEPHERD LOVES THE SHEEP.

It seems this should almost go without saying, but unfortunately love is not automatic in the Church these days.

We sling the word around freely; we think we know what it is, but in reality it has become too familiar of a word.

We will say "I love you" and "I love pizza" and not know the difference.

Let's look at two Greek words for love. The first one, of course, is *Agape*. It is used to describe the unconditional love God has for us. This is the kind of love we need to have for one another. The kind of love that lets the world know we are Jesus' disciples. John 13:35 says, *"By this all men will know that you are my disciples, if you love one another."*

Loving across the pews at church has to be more than a hand-shake or a fake hug. It has to be deeper. People outside the church can see when you're fake.

The second Greek word is *Phileo*, which means to have affection for someone. It is the *feeling* we get from love, and, unfortunately, it's the love most people know.

Church as we know it functions on this type of love. It is conditional and based on feelings we have for one another. We walk in love as long as our feelings are not altered. The first time you cause my feelings to be misplaced, I will abandon that love.

If we are going to show the world what true shepherding looks like, we are going to have to walk in agape (unconditional love).

The night before I got saved, Roger made an attempt to get me to go to church with him. He was in a church service with a well-known evangelist. The evangelist said that a drug addict from the east side of town was going to get saved. Roger immediately jumped up and headed to my house.

What Roger did not know is that I had been up for several days strung out on meth. I was lying on my parent's couch wishing and praying I could just go to sleep. After quite a few attempts at doing various other drugs to go to sleep, I found myself wide awake and miserable.

And there came Roger. Anybody but Roger, I thought. As he drove up and I realized it was him, dread hit me. I knew I was in for another onslaught of his telling me about how much I needed Jesus and how much Jesus loved me.

As soon as he entered the house, I made it known that I had had a bad day and was not in the mood for his pushy antics. That didn't seem to dissuade him. He began to preach with more fervor than usual, more passion seemed to flow through his veins. You would think I would have immediately given in, but it only made me madder.

At this point, I politely (can you hear the sarcasm?) told Roger to get the @#$%&^ out of my house and leave me the @#$%* alone. He said, "I'll leave, but I'm going to pray first." (Come on, seriously Roger!) And pray he did. When he finally got through ranting to God about my impending doom, he got up to leave. What happened next would forever change my life.

As he approached the door, he stopped, turned, and - with tears streaming down his cheeks - said these words, "I hope when I die and go to heaven, God blocks out my memory of you or it just won't be heaven."

My heart skipped a beat; I was in a state of shock. My heart of stone became jello in the hands of a merciful God. Never had anyone shown me that much love.

All I could think was how could he? I had spent the last year rejecting, cursing, and avoiding this pest who seemed undaunted by my rejections of him and his God.

Roger left that night without another word, only to return the next day prepared to do whatever it took to get me to that revival. Because of the love he showed the night before, my heart had no choice.

That night I found the love that Roger had showed me the previous evening. A sheep had reached out to a sheep with love and compassion, and a life that was once filled with darkness and gloom was now overflowing with hope.

4

THE NOMADIC SHEPHERD

The words that follow are not meant to offend in any way, but I do believe that we are faced with one of the greatest crises in the Church. An epidemic that if continued unchecked will cause continuous harm to the body of Christ.

I would like to address the nomadic shepherd. A nomadic shepherd is a shepherd who has no fields of his own. He just wanders from field to field looking for places to feed his sheep. A nomadic shepherd has no roots, no home, and no inheritance. He just wanders from place to place looking for food.

> **A nomadic shepherd has no roots, no home, and no inheritance. He just wanders from place to place looking for food.**

This paints a scary picture of the Church. How many sheep/shepherds do we see roaming from church to church looking for food? They have no home church; they have no inheritance in a house.

They are wandering vagabonds going from one house of worship to another house of worship.

That's what a nomad is by definition - a wandering vagabond, a homeless drifter. We all have our opinions of vagabonds or drifters. They are looked at with suspicion and distrust.

Think of the last time you saw a drifter walking down the street. He had his backpack slung over the shoulder. Everything about him seemed to be out of place. His hair was unkempt, his clothes were dirty and mismatched, and he looked like he had not shaved in a month of Sundays.

First off, don't go there. I'm not judging people or saying we should not minister to the homeless or the down and out. I'm just trying to paint a picture of a vagabond.

Your mind begins to wonder about who he could be and where he is from. If he had his thumb out to catch a ride, you had to weigh the compassion in you against the safety of your family. It's a no brainer who wins, right?

There are people in the Church like this. We have a spiritual term for them: church hoppers. They go from house to house, drifting from place to place. Let's see what the Word says about nomadic shepherds.

"Then Joseph said to his brothers and to his father's house-hold, 'I will go up and speak to Pharaoh and will say to him, "My brothers and my father's household, who were living

in the land of Canaan, have come to me. The men are shep-
herds; they tend livestock, and they have brought along their
flocks and herds and everything they own." When Pharaoh
calls you in and asks, "What is your occupation?" you
should answer, "Your servants have tended livestock from
our boyhood on, just as our fathers did." Then you will be
allowed to settle in the region of Goshen, for all shepherds
are detestable to the Egyptians.'" - Genesis 46:31-34

Here we find Jacob, who at the time was a nomadic shepherd. As a matter of fact, so were his father and grandfather. They all had the heart of a shepherd but none had a home. As long as they didn't have a home, their hearts couldn't flourish.

I didn't say they were not blessed; they were. They were very wealthy and very prosperous. Yet, none of them were satisfied. Why? They had everything but a place to settle.

How often do we see this in the Church? People who have the heart of the shepherd, but the Church never sees it fully because they have not got a place to call home. They are rich with the knowledge of Christ, they are wealthy with the gifts of the Spirit, but they are not satisfied because they have no home. How many have we seen who have the goods but you never see it because they have not stayed in one place long enough to be received? If you have a shepherd's heart, you have much to give, but you can't because you are nomadic.

How many revelations were taken to the grave because people didn't have anyone to share them with? How many sermons were never preached, how many healings would have taken place if people were not nomadic shepherds? Before we look further at Jacob, let's take a look at what the life of a nomadic shepherd entails.

1. INSTABILITY

Notice that in scripture the Church is referred to as a woman. In Rev. 19:9 and Rev. 21:9, the Church is referred to as the bride of Christ. A woman's greatest need is security. A woman can never be happy in a marriage without it. In all my years of pastoring, I have never counseled with a couple having marriage difficulty without addressing the security issue.

That's the same way it works in the church. That person sitting next to you can't receive from you because he does not see one who is stable. If someone sees that you are unstable in your relationship with the Lord or unstable in your worship or unstable in church attendance, why would he trust you?

When people walk through the back doors of our churches, they are looking for a place that they can feel secure. They are not looking for comfortable pews, air conditioners, or great programs. They're looking for security.

If you've ever seen a woman in an unsecure marriage, you know that all kinds of emotions surface. She can be shy and timid or brash and rude. She will be everything but normal. How many of you have been to churches and when you walked in the door the people were either shy and stay at a distance, or they were rude and snobbish? It's because there is no stability in the house provided by the shepherd in the pulpit or the shepherds in the pews.

Instability causes sheep to go looking for food. They think they are not getting fed at the church they are in so they run off to another church to eat. Because they have been taught instability, they will only stay in one place long enough to get food to sustain them on their journey to the next church.

When this occurs, it causes the sheep to eat an unbalanced diet of the Word. Now they crave only one kind of food. They go from church to church searching for the only food they like. They will go to one church because it's preaching on prosperity, but the moment it starts on servanthood they leave because servanthood doesn't fit their diet.

How many of us would just eat cake all the time? Eventually, as good as cake may be, it will cause our body to have an adverse effect.

The church should be growing based on a balanced diet of the Word of God. Don't leave a church because you see a change in the food. It may be that you've had enough of what you've been eating, and it's time to move on.

God has called us to be balanced Christians. You can't live your whole life eating dessert. Listen to the writer of Hebrews.

"Therefore let us leave the elementary teachings about Christ and go on to maturity, not laying again the foundation of repentance from acts that lead to death, and of faith in God, instruction about baptisms, the laying on of hands, the resurrection of the dead, and eternal judgment." - Hebrews 6:1-2

How many of us stay in elementary school in the Kingdom of God? We should be building up our faith, and not leaving when the teaching is different or hard. Of course, this puts a lot of responsibility on the pastor, doesn't it? We will touch on that more later.

2. CONFLICT

Notice the conflict between Abraham and Lot in Genesis.

"Now Lot, who was moving about with Abram, also had flocks and herds and tents. But the land could not support them while they stayed together, for their possessions were so great that they were not able to stay together. And quarreling arose between Abram's herdsmen and the herdsmen of Lot. The Canaanites and Perizzites were also living in the land at that time." - Genesis 13:5-7

The Bible records that both Abraham and Lot had great possessions, but great possessions do not rid you of conflict. The problem was they were nomadic shepherds, and nomadic shepherds are always in competition. Competition is the breeding ground for conflict.

Conflict in the body of Christ at times can't be helped, but unresolved conflict can be. Conflict that is unresolved will be carried on to the next house of worship.

Pastor Jones hurt your feelings when you were in the hospital by forgetting to come see you and pray with you before your surgery. You leave Pastor Jones' church and head down to Pastor Smith's church. Because you didn't deal with what happened at Pastor Jones' church, Pastor Smith gets the cold shoulder because you have unresolved conflict in your heart. Lo and behold, you're in the hospital once more. Pastor Smith can't make it, but he sends two of his Elders to pray with you. Because you still had hard feelings toward Pastor Jones, the Elders are not enough. You leave the hospital and leave the church to find a real pastor.

Thus begins a cycle of your running from church to church trying to find the perfect pastor, based on the one premise of their visiting you in the hospital.

When you don't deal with your conflict, you will introduce it to another church. This means that most churches are full of carry over conflicts that they didn't even have a part of.

I had a couple come to our church because they got hurt at another church. I counseled with them to resolve their conflict with the previous church. They said they dealt with it and were fine and ready to advance the Kingdom. Three months later another couple from that church showed up on our doorsteps. The first couple said they couldn't worship in the same house as the new couple. They both left the church. I just felt sorry for the next church they would attend. This is a cycle in the body of Christ that is played out over and over again.

Think of what happened to Lot. He wound up settling in a city that was full of wickedness, Sodom. How many people get involved in conflict and wind up in a place that is not God's will?

3. LONELINESS

There is nothing worse than seeing someone with no one; but, unfortunately, the nomadic lifestyle offers no lasting relationships. I truly believe that a nomad is scared of forming relationships that last because he would have to reveal his true heart, which would mean dealing with past hurts or mistakes.

It amazes me how many people will allow past hurts to keep them from experiencing the joys that can be found in lasting relationships.

We live in a world of iPods, iPads, texting, smart phones, Facebook, and Skype, yet we are lonelier than ever. Our relationships have become so surface, so general, that we don't really even know one another.

The shepherd's heart is the cure for this loneliness. If only we would give up our nomadic lifestyles and give up our need to roam, we could have relationships that last a lifetime.

Loneliness is not part of the Shepherd's heart lifestyle. I'm surrounded by hundreds of people that will still be in my life ten, twenty, and thirty years from now.

Listen, precious saint, loneliness is not cured overnight; it's cured over life. Relationships are cultivated over time. But if you will allow them to cultivate, you will walk in a sense of completeness like you could never imagine.

4. BITTERNESS

Chances are, if you're a nomadic shepherd, there is some bitterness inside you due to lack of forgiveness. Not forgiving someone is a weight that you don't have to carry. It's just too heavy.

Over the years I've come to realize that bitterness wears a mask to try to disguise itself. No one wants to be labeled as someone who struggles with bitterness.

Ponder with me if you would some of the disguises bitterness wears. How about sarcasm? Have you ever noticed someone who is sarcastic all the time? Listen to the verbiage they use. Chances are you will hear traces of a circumstance gone very badly. And given enough time, that person will share that bitterness with everyone around them.

How about signs of resentment toward a particular group of people? The choir director hurt you, so anybody who works with music has an evil hidden agenda. The Evangelist fell into open sin, so all Evangelists are perverts. We could go on and on.

Then there is the biggest disguise of all: the victim mentality. Everybody everywhere is out to get you. You see people around you and you assume they mean to do you harm. You've hidden your bitterness by thinking you've been damaged.

You think as long as you're a victim you have the right to remain bitter. You wander from church to church reliving all the things that caused you to be bitter. You keep all those events alive so you can hold on to your excuses for never trusting, and thus never becoming all that God wants you to be.

5. LOSS OF CONCERN FOR OTHER SHEEP

Eventually someone with a nomadic heart will lose concern for the sheep around them. His main concern will be for himself.

Let's go back to the verses we read in Genesis.

Gen 46:31 "Then Joseph said to his brothers and to his father's household, 'I will go up and speak to Pharaoh and will say to him, "My brothers and my father's house-

hold, who were living in the land of Canaan, have come to me. The men are shepherds; they tend livestock, and they have brought along their flocks and herds and everything they own." When Pharaoh calls you in and asks, "What is your occupation?" you should answer, "Your servants have tended livestock from our boyhood on, just as our fathers did." Then you will be allowed to settle in the region of Goshen, for all shepherds are detestable to the Egyptians.'"
- Genesis 46:31-34

Notice that Jacob was wandering in the Land of Canaan. If you will go back and look at the covenant that God made with Abraham, you will see that God told Abraham that He was going to give him that land. So why was Jacob *wandering* in a land he was supposed to be *settling* in?

Can you see this happening in the Church today? People wandering around *in* their promised land *looking for* their promised land? You may already be in the place you're supposed to be. Quit wandering from church to church and get settled. Stop complaining that you can't find your promised land. You may already be in it.

I understand trying to find the right church for you and your family. But if you've been to five churches in the last five years, then you're either a little too picky or you're too hard to please. Once you get in a church that has solid Word and good worship, you should stay until you either get a call from God to go to the mission field or you move to another state.

Nowhere in the Bible did people ever leave a church to help out a little church down the street. Nowhere in the Bible did people leave a church because they got mad at the pastor. Nowhere in the Bible did people leave because someone hurt their feelings. Nowhere in the Bible did people leave because they didn't get to teach a Sunday school class. Come on, people! When are we going to get planted so the Kingdom of God can truly advance? This whole wandering from church to church thing is getting old to God.

A person doesn't like something, and all of a sudden he gets "led" poisoning. He gets led to another church. You get shifted from your position at church and all of a sudden the pastor is out of the will of God.

I hear things like, "I'm here as long as you don't make a mistake." (No pressure!) The pastor is going to make a mistake. The direction of the church is going to be different than you thought. Deal with it. Listen to Paul's words:

"Obey your leaders and submit to their authority. They keep watch over you as men who must give an account. Obey them so that their work will be a joy, not a burden, for that would be of no advantage to you." - Hebrews 13:17

Most people can't handle the thought of someone being over them in the Kingdom of God, much less accepting the fact that you may be a burden to a pastor.

Every time you leave because of your pettiness, you add to the pastor's burdens. It's no wonder hundreds of pastors quit every Monday morning.

Now think of what your lack of concern does to the rest of the body of Christ. Every time you leave a church you take some of the heart of that church with you. You may not want to believe it, but you rip out some of that church's heart. You leave behind damaged scar tissue that will take many years to heal, if ever.

SETTLING WHERE THEY'RE NOT SUPPOSED TO

Next we find that Jacob had gone to Egypt. Why did he go to Egypt? He was already in the promised land. He left the promised land and went to the land of bondage. We see people do this. Things get a little hard, and they think somewhere else is better. Notice what the Word declares:

> *"You should answer, 'Your servants have tended livestock from our boyhood on, just as our fathers did.' Then you will be allowed to settle in the region of Goshen, for all shepherds are detestable to the Egyptians." - Genesis 46:34*

Shepherds were detestable to the Egyptians. Why would Jacob settle where his gifts and talents were detestable to the people? Do you see this happening in the Church? You leave a perfectly good church because there was a dry season. You go to a house that looks good, but what God has put in you, they not only don't need but don't like. This is a set up for further hurt, because now you try to change the people that refuse to change. They are not going to change into something they don't even like.

I had a member of my church leave because God had called them to go help a church and be an instrument of change. He/she felt like he/she needed to take our contemporary style of worship and show this other church how it was supposed to be done. Here's the problem with that: the person on the bottom is not the agent of change. Only the head has the power and authority to change. If the pastor likes the way it is, that's the way it is.

Notice that once they got to Egypt they became slaves. How many of us go someplace to serve, and they turn us into servants? You see there is a difference between wanting to serve and someone making a slave out of you. Someone who wants to serve flows out of a shepherd's heart, but a slave is in bondage.

Do you realize that as long as you are wandering your shepherd's heart is worthless? I believe that this is a detestable cycle in the Kingdom of God. Think of it this way: a nomadic shepherd is like the servant who hid his talent. He had resources to do great things for his master but decided to hide them. If you're wandering around and around, no one will ever see your true talent.

SO WHAT DO WE DO TO STOP THE NOMADIC CYCLE IN THE KINGDOM OF GOD?

1. SETTLE IN A PLACE WHERE YOUR HEART CAN BE MOST EFFECTIVE.

Settle means just that: settle. How many of you remember your mother telling you, "Get somewhere and settle down"? She meant that you were to sit down and stay there. That's what the Spirit of the Lord is saying to the Church.

How dumb does it look for you to invite your co-worker to church for the fifth time and you give them directions to yet another church? Sounds silly, but it happens.

Now let me get to the heart of the matter. This is where I'm going to make some pastors mad. At Voice to the Nations, I'm settled. I've told my church and everyone who will listen. I will never leave Voice to the Nations. My congregation knows that I will marry them and bury them. I will never take a bigger church that offers me more money, and I have had offers. I will not leave until Jesus stops giving me a voice; however He chooses to do that.

This has given my church a sense of security. Because I'm not going anywhere, they can trust me. Now understand what I'm about to tell you. People go from church to church because they are following the example of the leaders of those churches. A pastor will go from church to church and expect the people of those churches to stay put.

Why should they? The pastors don't. They bail out on the people, so the people bail out on the pastor. If the pastor is not in it to win it, then why should the people be? Why should the people get close to their leaders if they are going to leave them and carry their secrets with them? Who wants to confide in someone you know will be gone in two years? Do you realize most pastors stay only an average of about five years? After five years they run out of things to preach so they want to go to another church so they can re-preach those same old sermons again.

When I first started pastoring, I remember asking a seasoned pastor one time how I could keep a fresh word for my house? His response broke my heart. He said, "Just pull out a sermon you preached last year, change the text and title, and preach it again." No wonder people leave churches. When are we as pastors going to get serious about our calling? People would be far more likely to be planted in one house if the men and women of God kept a fresh Word and stayed put.

I know there are exceptions to the rule. A pastor runs into a deacon-run church that refuses to go anywhere. A pastor steps in for a season to hold things together while waiting on the steady pastor, etc. But I don't think this is the majority.

Think of all the great mega-churches in America, and notice what they all have in common. Think about Apostle Ron Carpenter, Bishop T.D. Jakes, Pastor Rod Parsley, Pastor Joel Osteen, Pastor Rick Warren, Pastor Bill Hybels, Pastor Ed Young, and Bishop Eddie Long, just to name few. What do they all have in common? They don't leave. Every one of them have been in it for the long haul. Now I know that there are faithful men and women of God who served years in smaller, less known churches, but the principle is the same in both cases. People will trust a pastor who is there to stay.

Pastors who are in it for the long haul show their people what it means to endure the process. How can you expect people to endure the problems they face if the pastor is not willing to endure it with them? I get weary of hearing people say they will never get close to a pastor again because they know the pastor will leave them eventually. I have people in my church I have never even met before, but they have a sense of security in the fact that I will never go anywhere.

In order for you to be most effective, you have to be committed to stay. In order to be committed to stay, you must take out all options for leaving.

We all know that options are made to be taken. If you have an option to bail out, you will eventually take it. At Voice to the Nations, I removed every option I ever had to leave. All my colleagues know that I'm in it to win it, so they don't approach me. My family knows

I'm in it to win it, so they don't expect me to go anywhere. I've stood before my congregation and told them I'll never leave, and every time we have new members join I reiterate that fact to them.

Now it doesn't matter if you're the pastor of a church or a layman, you have to remove all options for leaving.

I hear options like, "I'm here until the Lord leads me away." There's way too much "led" poisoning in the church. (I know it's the second time you've heard that in this book). God doesn't lead people away from churches unless it's to pursue the purposes of God and, even then, we better be careful and use discernment. Hurt feelings or bad attitudes are almost always the reason someone leaves. Here's a popular option people like to take. "I'll be here until the Lord opens another door for me." How many doors does God open for some people? Some walk through more doors than an elevator attendant. I wonder how many doors actually get kicked down. What about the option of, "I'm going to go where I'm needed." No, you want to go where you can be seen. You're needed right where you are. It's just not out front, so you want to find a place where you're seen out front. You may be tempted to use the option of, "I want to go where I can use my talents." More than likely you don't want to go through the process of waiting until you've proven yourself.

At Voice to the Nations we look at people's hearts, not at their talents or skill sets. We make people go through the same process to do ministry no matter how talented they are. We've discovered very talented people in our midst, but they didn't have the heart of the shepherd so they left mad because we didn't use them week one.

The bottom line is if you are looking for an excuse to leave, you will find one. Stop looking, and stay put!

2. FORGET PAST CHURCH EXPERIENCES.

We start thinking about all the times we settled in a church and got hurt. It's hard to put past hurts behind us, but it's the only way we can become all that God wants us to be. How long is your past going to direct your future?

If you have any clue about relationships, you would know that there will be times of hurt. You can't avoid getting hurt. When we serve together, worship together, sing together, and minister together, there will be times when we hurt one another. No matter how hard we try, we are going to let our agendas and our desires get in the way of doing ministry.

Whenever flesh is present, there will be hurt feelings. Imagine how tragic it is in the Kingdom of God for someone who sings in the choir to get mad because he/she didn't get the solo he/she deserved. Notice I said deserved. You may very well have deserved the honor more, but to allow that hurt to rule your life is crazy. Do you not know that God will bless you in His timing not in yours?

What we often look at as hurt is actually God making sure we're in it for the right reasons. Chances are, the person who hurt you not only didn't mean to but didn't even know it. I remember when I was just starting out in ministry. Our pastor had to have surgery on his throat and could not preach for three months. Those of us in leadership got our chance to preach. Oh, what a great day it was! Another leader and I preached back to back Sundays. The other leader got a love offering of $50.00, and I didn't get anything. My wife and I got our feelings hurt. I thought, did I do that bad of a job? I mean $50.00 wasn't a lot of money, but it was the principle of the thing.

I had a choice: I could stay mad, get over it, or deal with it. Staying mad was not an option because I just don't like being mad at someone. Getting over it was not an option because unresolved issues build up to form major problems in one's life. So I chose to deal with it. As soon as my pastor could talk again, I asked him (a lot of stuff could be solved this way) why did the other leader get paid and I didn't? He was so upset. He thought I did get paid. The church clerk simply forgot to write me a check. I could have let hard feelings keep me from having a relationship with the greatest man I've ever known. Past hurts have to stay where they belong, in the past.

Let me take a moment to talk about what to do with these hurts as they arise. Deal with them. Don't let hurt feelings develop into a hurt relationship. One little thing never destroyed a relationship. It's always the accumulation of a lot of little things. All of a sudden, one little thing turns into two, and then to three. The next thing you know, everything that person does is under a microscope and you only see the frustrating things that person does. If this is where you are, then you've let things go too far. You may need to back up to a happier time in your relationship. When you do, you will see the joy that relationship has brought you, instead of just seeing all the frustrating details.

3. GIVE UP YOUR FREEDOM TO ROAM.

You can't roam from pasture to pasture and expect God to use you. People will only allow a stranger to minister to them for so long. I truly believe the more someone gets to know you, the greater you will be able to minister to him/her.

The grass is never greener on the other side. The church down the road doesn't have it like you think they do. Every church in the world has its issues. Issues are not your excuse to bail out on the church and the man of God. Deal with issues and you will find you're already in a great church. Giving up the freedom to roam is removing all options; you're locked in.

I can always tell when someone comes in the church that just roams about in the Kingdom of God. They make statements like, "I am here to help you." Do I look like I need help? Am I struggling to the point that God has pulled you away from helping out another pastor to come and rescue me? Come on, are you for real?

What about the guy who comes in and says, "I am here for a season." My goodness, I hope it's a short season.

We don't need people who roam. They cause strife, confusion, and disunity. Their purpose is to rip apart not hold together. If you are someone who roams from church to church, stop! You do not have the heart of the great Shepherd and you do not have the people's best interest in mind. You are full of your own agenda, and you need to settle even if it does mean you don't get to be out front.

Vagabonds are afraid to settle because they may have to deal with some issues. You see, as long as you are roaming, you're never anywhere long enough for people to see your faults. The moment you get to a place where God can start to minister to you through someone else, you're gone. (And you will even use your war cry, "I've been hurt.")

As long as someone roams, he has no accountability; no one is holding him to his word or actions. He can do what he pleases; and if he messes up, no problem, he was leaving anyway.

I'm amazed at how we will criticize the woman who doesn't like to give up her front row seat where she has sat for thirty years. At least she's been there! Why give up her seat to someone who is just going to be gone in a couple of weeks anyway?

5

UNDERSTANDING PARTNERSHIP

"I thank my God every time I remember you. In all my prayers for all of you, I always pray with joy because of your partnership in the gospel from the first day until now, being confident of this, that He who began a good work in you will carry it on to completion until the day of Christ Jesus. It is right for me to feel this way about all of you, since I have you in my heart; for whether I am in chains or defending and confirming the gospel, all of you share in God's grace with me. God can testify how I long for all of you with the affection of Christ Jesus. And this is my prayer: that your love may abound more and more in knowledge and depth of insight, so that you may be able to discern what is best and may be pure and blameless until the day of Christ, filled with the fruit of righteousness that comes through Jesus Christ-to the glory and praise of God." -Philippians 1:3-11 { NIV }

So far we have covered shepherds, sheep, wolves, and hired hands. In order to truly understand the Shepherd's heart, you have to understand the message in the pages that follow. The foundation of everything in the Kingdom of God begins with partnership.

How many of us have been in a church service and heard the minister say the words, "He that began a good work in you will bring it to completion"? This statement is always followed by a few people shouting, "Amen!" This is always an encouraging scripture.

But the problem is we cut the promise a little short. Notice in verse six of Philippians one, Paul said, *"being confident of this."* Being confident of what? Paul was able to boldly make this statement about God's completing the work in his Philippian brothers and sisters, because of the confidence he had in their partnership in the gospel.

You need to understand: if you want the complete plan of God to come to pass in your life, then you're going to have to understand partnership. How many of us know those who would say they don't need the church or anybody else for that matter, all they need is the Lord. I'm sorry, but just you and Jesus having your own thing going is not going to cut it.

I believe the Bible is very clear that it is not God's will for man to be alone. From Adam to us, God has never desired His children to be alone in the work He has for us. Look at this passage of scripture.

"Again I saw something meaningless under the sun: There was a man all alone; he had neither son nor brother. There was no end to his toil, yet his eyes were not content with his wealth. 'For whom am I toiling,' he asked, 'and why am I depriving myself of enjoyment?' This too is meaningless- a miserable business! two are better than one, because they have a good return for their work: If one falls down, his friend can help him up. But pity the man who falls and has no one to help him up! Also, if two lie down together, they will keep warm. But how can one keep warm alone? Though one may be overpowered, two can defend themselves. A cord of three strands is not quickly broken." -Ecclesiastes 4:7-12

Notice being alone is just too much work. Why try to go at this thing alone if it is so much work? When the enemy of my soul attacks, it would be nice to have

> **When the enemy of my soul attacks, it would be nice to have someone standing with me.**

someone standing with me. Let me go ahead and say something bold. If you don't have someone that you have partnered with in the gospel, then you will never see God do a complete work in your life.

I believe this is why so many people in the Kingdom of God are not seeing the fruit they desire, because they are going at it alone. God will complete the good work He has for you, but He will use partnership to do it. In reality, the statement "God will complete the good work He began in you" is dead without partnership.

There are so many who reject this idea of partnership. They use the statement, "A man can only depend on God." In depending on God, you need to know that He will use others to fight by your side. How do you think God sends help? He uses others to help us in our time of trouble. If we have close partnerships with others, then that's who God is going to send to our rescue.

WHY PARTNERSHIP?

Ask yourself why someone wouldn't want to commit to this type of partnership. It will usually be a reason like *I've been hurt too many times before.* Getting hurt is a part of life, and I don't want to belittle your hurt, but get your healing and move on. I'm sorry, but the Kingdom of God is bigger than our hurts. As long as you stay hurt with someone, you will never be effective. Don't let past hurts make you miss out on future positive relationships. It's too easy to let past hurts keep us from experiencing all that God has for us.

How many people have missed out on what God had for them because they were busy playing the victim? People tend to lean towards the victim mentality because it's easier, and you get

> **It's too easy to let past hurts keep us from experiencing all that God has for us.**

attention. It's easier to walk around flashing your scars than it is to just forgive and move on.

Another reason people don't want to partner is because of pride. People get the mentality that they can do it on their own. If they acknowledged that they needed a partner, then they would be acknowledging weakness. We can't mistake wisdom for weakness. It's a wise man who will say, "I can't do this alone; I need a partner in the faith to walk it out with me."

When I first gave my heart to the Lord, I thought I was so strong in the Lord that I didn't need others to pray or be there for me. When people offered to pray for me, I would tell them that God heard me and I didn't need their prayers. Dumb, right? What I did was the extreme, and I paid an extreme price for my arrogance. Not long after I got saved and thought I was super Christian, I fell back into sin because I thought I could do it on my own. You see, I was delivered from a life of drugs and alcohol. I was a full blown drug addict by the age of thirteen. So when I say I backslid, that's what I slid back into. Now my case may seem like the extreme, but I believe there are many Christians who, on one level or another, let pride keep them from partnering with others in the faith, and this keeps them from truly stepping into God's complete work for their life.

Some would say the idea of partnership is great for some, but "I'm a loner." Well, the fact is everybody can relate to someone. Have you ever meet a happy hermit? No! They are always grumpy old men. They're grumpy because they are trying to go at it alone.

Even people who are loners don't like to be by themselves all the time. No matter how alone someone may like to be, or how much of an introvert someone is, there will come a day when he needs someone to stand with him.

I've noticed one of the biggest reasons people don't want to partner is they don't want people to know who they really are. They think they will not be accepted for who they are. Low self-esteem is a mean devil that stops so many from reaching their full potential.

This leads to the really cool thing about partnership. Partnership allows you to be the best "you" you can be. Sometimes we just need someone to bring out the best in us.

I remember when I first felt the call to ministry. I was young, uneducated, an ex-drug addict, an ex-convict, and suffered from low self-esteem, but I had a partner in the gospel come on the scene. Pastor Perry Keyt would look at me with such promise. He would tell me how great I was going to be and how much potential I had until one day I actually thought he might be right. Don't get me wrong, I had my amazing bride telling me how great I was, but I thought that was her job. (By the way, she's the most incredible support a man could ever want.) Now, here was a man whom I aspired to be like telling me I was going to do great exploits. At the time, I didn't even know what the word *exploits* meant!

This may mean somewhere down the line you may have to change a little, but everybody has to change every now and then. I did. I had to rise up and meet the expectations my pastor put on me.

At the time my pastor was telling me those things, I could barely read or write. Now you're reading a book I wrote. God used a partner - a person in my life - to perfect His plan in me.

PARTNERSHIP PRODUCES ACCOUNTABILITY

Something happens to you when you allow someone in your heart: it changes you. When you know someone is looking to you for help, it will cause you to come up higher. I am surrounded by people who depend on the partnership that we have together.

Now I could do one of two things: I could worry that my every move would be judged, or I could make sure my every move was above judgment. It's not about someone judging you; it's about

> **When you know someone is looking to you for help, it will cause you to come up higher.**

someone loving you. Paul said, "*It's right for me to feel this way since I have you in my heart.*" Paul loved his partners in the faith, but we will get to that deeper in a moment.

Partnership not only allows you to have help in times of need, but it will also keep you accountable to someone. It seems in the Church today we fight against accountability, when we should be embracing it. When we are accountable to a partner in the faith, sin and circumstance tend to shrink.

I have found there to be two enemies of accountability. The first is pride. So many people are too prideful to admit that they need someone else to help them in life. When we remove the hand of accountability from our lives, we remove the very hand of God from our lives.

If God is calling you to another level, whom do you think is going to lift you up? It's the power of partnership that will catapult you to your next stage in life. Don't reject the plan of God, but rather embrace it. Let me go ahead and release you. It's okay to need someone else to give you a lift in life. There's no shame in needing a hand in life. Accountability is that hand.

You came into this life needing a doctor to catch you, a parent to hold your hand, and someone to help you ride a bike for the first time. We could go on all day about how many times you've needed someone to partner with you in life. What makes you think that serving the Lord is any different?

The second enemy of accountability is selfishness. We think that if we allow someone to hold us accountable then we will have to hold them accountable, and we don't want to take the time to be our brother's keeper. I'm happy to inform you that you are your brother's keeper. It is your responsibility to make sure your brother is accountable in this life. Sometimes I think it is easier to receive correction than it is to give it. In partnership, God will often call on you to do the difficult things, and I can't think of anything more difficult than confrontation. Confronting a brother is part of what we have to do as partners. It is never fun, but more often than not, it is very necessary.

I take great pride in the leaders I have at Voice to the Nations. They are very balanced in their ministry approach. This balance comes because they are not afraid to allow me to confront them on issues that need to be dealt with. Lack of confrontation in a ministry or in a person's life will cause lumps to build up underneath the carpet of your life. If those lumps are not dealt with, you will eventually trip over them.

Now, I'm not talking about those people out there who love confronting others on their shortcomings but never want anyone to address their own character flaws. People of this nature tend to like to divert attention off them so no one notices their qualities that are unbecoming of a Christian. They don't desire partnerships; they are instigators in the Kingdom and need to be confronted themselves.

THE SOURCE OF PARTNERSHIP

"It is right for me to feel this way about all of you, since I have you in my heart; for whether I am in chains or defending and confirming the gospel, all of you share in God's grace with me." - Philippians 1:7

We need to realize that there is one thing that gives us the right to partnership, and that is love. The first rule of partnership is this:

you have to love the person that you're partnering with. You have no right to partnership until you have someone in your heart first. When someone is in your heart and there is a deep-seated love for him/her, no matter what he/she says or does you can never turn on him/her. Remember Jesus died for you at your worst moment.

It seems in the Kingdom of God we have more acquaintances than we do partners. You see an acquaintance will only know your name, but a partner will understand your motives. Of course, that's the whole problem with partnership: we don't want people

> **The whole problem with partnership is we don't want people to get close enough to get to know our true motives.**

to get close enough to know our true motives. As a partner, you can never let someone in your heart until you know his/her motives. How many people have you known that got hurt because someone with wrong motives was in their heart? Partnership is all about standing up for someone and fighting for someone, and that's hard to do if there is no trust. So here's a question for you: whose heart are you in? If there is no one or only a few who you know have let you into their heart, then you may need to check your motives.

Transparency is one of the scariest things in the world. It allows someone to see things that you don't want him to see, but here is what I've discovered: when I'm transparent, I'm free. You see me in my rawest form, and you love me anyway.

We've all been hurt in the Body of Christ, because it's full of people, but that can never be our excuse for not loving again. How often do we see people who hide behind the fact that they have been

> **Can you see me in my rawest form and love me anyway?**

hurt before? We've all heard it, "I can't let someone in. You don't know how badly I was hurt." Unfortunately, "I've been hurt" has become the Church's war cry. Is that not the saddest thing ever? If only we in the Church could understand that once we sort out the hurts, we will find partnerships that will last a lifetime.

Bottom line: we've all been hurt, but that's no license to stop loving people.

Several years ago, I went through a series of rough patches in my ministry that caused me to become calloused and hard. I built up such a distrust towards people that it started to affect my ministry.

Pastor Keyt invited me up to a pastors' conference his church was hosting. On the drive up, my wife, who is the love of my life and my biggest fan, proceeded to tell me that she felt I had lost my love for the people. As you could imagine, I was both shocked and appalled. That night Bishop Jim Bolin began to preach a message. The title of his message was "How to Fall Back in Love with Your Church". My wife was right as usual, and God got my attention that night. I crumbled to the floor weeping and seeking God's forgiveness because I had let the wrong people dictate my love for the right people.

At my church, Voice to the Nations (the greatest group of people in the world; forgive my shameless plug), I have been hurt many times, but through those hurts I have found partners who will blow out the fires of hell for me.

One Saturday we were having a work day at church. As we stood in the foyer of the church, we were talking on the issue of gossip and what a negative impact it has on the church. One of the young men standing there was Tommy, who happens to be one of my best friends.

First, let me say that Tommy is as thick as an oak tree and can bench press a truck. On top of that he's a boxer. At the same time, he has a heart of gold and more integrity than anyone I know. This guy truly is the real deal.

Tommy said with a tear running down his cheek, "Pastor, I don't know what I would do if I heard someone talking about you." I know what I would do if I were the one that gossiped. Run!

At that moment in time, I realized that every hurt I had endured was worth it to have a partner like that. Every person who ever trashed me to make themselves look good, every person who lied to try to destroy my reputation didn't matter. I had a partner in the gospel that was real. I understood what Solomon meant.

"A man of many companions may come to ruin, but there is a friend who sticks closer than a brother." - Proverbs 18:24

At that moment, Tommy showed me the heart of Jesus, the heart of a shepherd.

Recently, my church and another church merged. Most pastors get scared to death at the thought of a merger with another church, as were we. But Pastor Keith Ford (one of the most amazing men of God in the world) trusted the heart that was in me to lead not only my congregation but his as well. It has been a near perfect partnership. When I think of Pastor Keith and all he has sacrificed for the Kingdom of God, I can't help but think it's all worth it.

You see Pastor Keith didn't just join our church, he took a big risk. He gave up his role as leader of a great church. We didn't merge with a struggling church; we merged with a church that was doing great and had a clear vision.

Pastor Keith's heart for the city was so big that he gave up his right as leader to partner with me so together we could have a greater impact on our community.

No heartbreak I could ever go through could match the joy that my partnership with Pastor Keith brings me.

Here's a challenge for you. Do you have stories of people in your life that you can say you have partnerships with on a level that deep?

SHARING: THE PURPOSE OF PARTNERSHIP

"For whether I am in chains or defending and confirming the gospel, all of you share in God's grace with me." - Philippians 1:7b

As if that scripture is not enough, we find verses like:

"Carry each other's burdens, and in this way you will fulfill the law of Christ" - Galatians 6:2

"Now if we are children, then we are heirs-heirs of God and co-heirs with Christ, if indeed we share in his sufferings in order that we may also share in his glory." - Romans 8:17

Sometimes we are called to carry burdens that are not ours and sufferings that we didn't ask for, but it's all part of walking in partnership. Joys and sorrows, happiness and sadness, ups and downs. They all have to be shared.

Think of sports. If a baseball team wins the World Series, they come running out of the dugout celebrating together. Even in individual sports, a runner coming across the finish line wants someone there to celebrate with him. In life it's the same way. We want people who will celebrate our victories with us. I think the worst possible thing that could happen to someone is to be on a golf course and get a hole-in-one, but there is no one around to see it. No one to celebrate with.

At the same time, when we come up a little short in life, or even just blow it big time, we want someone present to help us up. We want someone there for the good, the bad, and the ugly. We need partnership because we need someone to share with us.

We need to realize that partnership is a two headed coin. You can't expect someone to share with you if you're not willing to share with someone. It's easy to reach up and need a hand, but what about the day when there is a hand reaching up to you for help? Whom do we know in a lopsided relationship? One person does all the work

> **It's easy to reach up and need a hand, but what about the day when there is a hand reaching up to you for help?**

to keep it alive and the other just does his/her own thing. In the Kingdom of God it's give and take, not take and take some more.

Remember: love your neighbor as you would yourself. Wow, what a concept! It's the second greatest commandment but the most neglected.

People don't like what I'm talking about because they associate partnership with words like submitting, depending, and honoring.

AFFECTION: THE DRIVE OF PARTNERSHIP

"God can testify how I long for all of you with the affection of Christ Jesus." - Philippians 1:8

Is there a longing in your heart when you are away from the saints of God? My wife and I can go on vacation and by the fifth day we want to get back to church so we can be with our congregation. I can't tell you how many vacations we've cut short so we could get home to be with our church family. As a matter of fact, we plan most of our vacations so we don't have to miss more than one service. Why? Because we have a deep affection for each and every one of them. Ask yourself this question. Do I truly miss my church family when I'm away? If the answer is "No" or "I don't know" then you most likely don't have a deep affection for your church family. If you can miss multiple services with no problem, then you probably lack affection for your fellow church members. This is where most people fall off into their "poor me" scenario. They say, "Nobody has affection for me, and that's why I don't have enough affection for anybody else." If you wish people at your church were more affectionate toward you, then you may be the answer. Why don't you try being the moving force of affection in your church? They may not be affectionate because you're not. Never use someone else as your excuse to miss out on the greatest pleasure in the Kingdom of God, the pleasure of affectionate partnership.

That person you've never taken the time to get to know may be the key to your destiny. You never know when a godly friendship, full of affection, can lead to greatness. I never dreamed the day I met my pastor and friend Perry Keyt that, because of our affectionate partnership, I would one day pastor a great church myself. You need to understand the first time I saw Pastor Keyt. I was intimidated to say the least. He stood 6'10" and carried an anointing that stood

> **You never know when a godly friendship, full of affection, can lead to greatness.**

taller than his height. I could have let fear and intimidation overcome me and stayed at a distance, but I took a chance. Who am I kidding? He took the chance. But isn't that what it's all about: taking a chance. Because of that chance, Pastor Keyt pushed me to greatness. He was not always nice and gentle, but because of his affection toward me, I always knew he had the Kingdom's best interest in mind. Today, my pastor is no longer with us, but I still long to be in his presence. Because of the partnership we formed, in times of need and on the heels of great accomplishments, I still reach for the phone to call him. I long for him to pour into me and to encourage me. Oh, how I miss that partnership. We used to talk regularly, and my heart would leap when I heard his voice. Only when you develop an affection for someone can they truly drive you to greatness.

Our church started a work in Kenya. The pastors of the church are Samuel and Jackie. Before they began the work they came to

America and spent a couple of months experiencing our church so they could duplicate it. During their stay with us, a deep affection was formed between us as well as our entire congregation.

We spent a great deal of time together, sharing laughter and tears. We got to know one another on a deep level. I was able to see the heart he truly possessed.

I can't wait every year to go over and spend time with them. Samuel always quotes Proverbs 25:25, *"Like cold water to a weary soul is good news from a distant land."* He understands that when I come I will deposit something into our partnership. I always look forward to hearing him quote that verse right before I get up to speak.

In 2007, Kenya had an election that went very badly, especially in the city of Eldoret, the location of one of our churches. Our pastors had to flee the city to get out of harm's way as the people were rioting. Here in the states, we began to earnestly pray. We were so brokenhearted over their tragedy.

Because of our partnership, we were able to minister to this beautiful couple from ten thousand miles away. So deep is the affection we have for one another, I could almost feel their pain.

DEPTH DEPENDS ON PARTNERSHIP

"And this is my prayer: that your love may abound more and more in knowledge and depth of insight." - Philippians 1:9

We've all seen them. Shallow Christians. They are men and women who love God, but are at best immature in their walk with Christ. Usually, the reason they are so immature is because they are out trying to do their own thing.

You know the ones I'm talking about. They have all the potential, but they never seem to become all that God wants them to be. A spiritual loner will never receive from God on the level of a person who has partnership. Get out your spiritual radar and find a mature Christian. Notice his attributes: faithful to one church, consistent in his relationships, and serves his pastor faithfully. We all desire a deeper understanding as well as a deeper walk, but it will never happen if we've not partnered with other saints of God. Look at the next verse:

"So that you may be able to discern what is best and may be pure and blameless until the day of Christ." - Philippians 1:10

One of the greatest weaknesses in the Church today is our lack of discernment. Why is this the case? There's no depth of knowledge, because there's no depth of partnership.

Without a greater understanding of who God is, we can't discern what God's will is. We can't have a greater understanding until we understand what it means to partner with other saints of God.

Ask yourself these questions. Why do I want great revelations from God? For what purpose do I want to go deeper into the mind and heart of God? Even if you were so egocentric that you wanted people to see how much of God you knew, you would still need someone to hear that revelation.

We have people in the body of Christ who claim to walk so closely with God they should be glowing. In reality, they are no closer to God than the most immature of Christians. Why? There is no one in their life that they have partnered with. No one holds them accountable, no one speaks into their life, and they have yet to be transparent enough to truly have a partnership.

So let's challenge your heart. How often do you get a revelation from God? Is your revelation centered on you or the Body of Christ? Do you seek to know God more for yourself or for others?

6

FELLOWSHIP BEYOND FRIED CHICKEN

If you've been in or around the church for a while, you will know about the pot luck suppers and covered dish dinners. This is where all the ladies of the church cook their Sunday best. If you are from the South, there are always several plates of fried chicken. You can look on every plate, and you will see it: a leg a, thigh, a wing, or a breast. People sit around eating their chicken and "fellowship-ping". We all like to eat and fellowship. It's a part of church life, even today. I believe we think it's the only thing we can do together without sinning.

After church, a group will head to the restaurant uptown, and another group will go a restaurant downtown. I remember when we first started Voice to the Nations. We had a 3:00 p.m. service on Sunday because we were in a borrowed church. We would all go out to eat after church and be able to sit at one table. The whole church would sit at one table. Those were hard times as the church goes, but we did have great fellowship after church, and still do, just on a much larger scale.

The problem is the fellowship didn't go beyond the fried chicken we were eating. We had shallow conversations and not very meaningful dialogue. We talked of sports and weather or work related issues. On occasion we may discuss the sermon and the music. A couple of times we talked about where we would be one day (that was pretty cool). But for the most part it was superficial. I believe God is calling the Church to a much deeper level of fellowship.

If you're truly sold out to a house and to the people of that house, you will know what I mean by what I'm about to say. There are times when I just miss being around God's people. As I've said before, my wife and I can be on vacation and leave a day or two early just so we can get home to see our people. There seems to be a deep-seated need in our lives to be in fellowship with each other. If you feel this at times, you have a shepherd's heart trying to reveal itself.

It's okay to have a longing to be around the people of God. At Voice to the Nations, our whole lives revolve around each other. Many of our people are much closer to each other than they are with their own families. This happens when a relationship is built on a deeper level than fried chicken.

The Greek word for fellowship is *koinonia*. It means partnership or to have in common with. In the Kingdom of God, we all have something in common: our faith. It links us together eternally. It is the common denominator for every believer.

When we go to Africa for our mission trips, we have nothing in common with most of the people we meet. We don't like the same foods, we don't like same clothes, we don't like to live in the same kind of houses, and we don't speak the same language. But once I mention the name of Jesus, we begin to have fellowship because Jesus becomes our common denominator. We may have to use an interpreter, but we have fellowship.

I truly believe we draw strength from one another. If I'm fellowshipping and sharing the things I have in common with others, my spirit man, as well as my heart, take encouragement.

Have you ever noticed people who have fellowship with others seem to have a deeper relationship and fellowship with God? We, as a family of God, need to realize that we need one another. Some would say they don't have anything to offer, but we all have things to offer. As a church, we need to be imparting into one another the things that God has imparted into us. It's wrong for you to hold back anything God has given you. Let me give you an example.

"Likewise, teach the older women to be reverent in the way they live, not to be slanderers or addicted to much wine, but to teach what is good. Then they can train the younger women to love their husbands and children." - Titus 2:3-4

I wonder how many Godly women are imparting into the lives of the young ladies. If you look at the generation of young ladies that are coming up, you would say not many.

It's hard for us to judge the next generation if we are not influencing them with our fellowship. It's amazing what a conversation can do to help a young person take a different path. We think they don't listen, but they do. And if they are not listening, it may be because we are not saying anything worth hearing. And the times we do say something, it's in a judgmental way.

Are we trashing them or fellowshipping with them? If we talk *to* them instead of talking *at* them, we may make a difference. Sorry, let me get off my soap box.

When I impart into someone, I'm taking the relationship beyond fried chicken, but imparting will require you to take responsibility for *what* you impart. That's why so few people take the time to deposit things into other's lives. You will have to live up to what you impart. If you tell a young lady to act like a young lady, you will have to act like a lady. If you tell a young man to act like a gentleman, then he better not see you acting like a jerk to your wife.

Over the course of our marriage, my wife and I have had times where we disagreed on matters. In that course of time, we have never raised our voices at one another nor have our kids ever seen us act rudely toward one another. Never. Consequently, when my son got married, he and his bride never raise their voices or act rudely toward each other. My wife and I live up to what we imparted.

We need to realize that in order for us to have this true fellowship, we will need to connect with the people around us. Connection comes when you find that common denominator or common ground. Let's look at some areas that we have common ground.

WE ARE FIGHTING THE SAME DEVIL.

"Be self-controlled and alert. Your enemy the devil prowls around like a roaring lion looking for someone to devour. Resist him, standing firm in the faith, because you know that your brothers throughout the world are undergoing the same kind of sufferings." - 1 Peter 5:8-9

Just because we don't fight the same demons doesn't mean we don't fight the same devil. Let me show you what I mean.

We think that because someone is not fighting in the same area that we are fighting he/she can't understand our problem. One person is fighting addiction and another person is fighting lust. One person is fighting poverty and another person is fighting rebellious children. These are four different attacks, but they are by the same devil.

The enemy will attack two saints with two different problems and then use the fact that they're fighting two different demons to bring discord. It's amazing how someone can struggle with smoking cigarettes and judge someone who is struggling with alcohol. They are two different addictions but the same devil. How about the teenager who is trying to fit in so she's struggling with having sex and the senior saint gossiping about her? They both are struggling with a sin, and that sin is causing discord in the church. What would happen if we forget about the different demons and focus on the same devil? What if we started fighting for one another instead of fighting each other? Imagine what would happen if in a moment of true fellowship the person who smoked and person who drank came together and fought each other's demons. What if, at a point of pure connection, that senior saint and that teenager helped each other with their struggles with gossip and sex? I truly believe this is the shepherd's heart in action.

The truth of the matter is we've accepted *our* struggle; we understand it. But we may not understand *their* struggle, and we fear what we do not understand.

I have the great privilege to minster to some of the greatest ex-addicts and ex- all around bad people you could ever meet. The reason I can minister to them is because I don't judge their battles; I fight with them. Even in areas I can't relate.

I have no problem relating to the drug addict because I used to be one. But just because I've never had an abortion does not mean I can't minister to one who has. It's the same devil attacking in different ways. It's not our job to focus on what they're fighting; it's our job to fight.

WE HAVE THE GIFTS IN COMMON.

"Now to each one the manifestation of the Spirit is given for the common good. To one there is given through the Spirit the message of wisdom, to another the message of knowledge by means of the same Spirit, to another faith by the same Spirit, to another gifts of healing by that one Spirit, to another miraculous powers, to another prophecy, to another distinguishing between spirits, to another speaking in different kinds of tongues, and to still another the interpretation of tongues. All these are the work of one and the same Spirit, and he gives them to each one, just as he determines." - 1 Corinthians 12:7-11

The Bible makes it clear that there are different gifts, but there is the common ground of gifts. All the gifts are given to the Church for the common good.

Here's what I've found. The gifts seem to flock together. If someone has the gift of prophecy, he will go to a church where everyone operates in the gift of prophecy. If someone walks in the gift of healing, he will go to a church whose primary focus is on healing. But this brings imbalance in the Kingdom of God. If every gift is flocking together, then the church is missing the gifts collectively.

What would happen if the gifts were all operating in the same house with each gift waiting for its moment to be used? The one who operates in the gift of prophecy waits until his gift is needed. The one who walks in the gift of healing waits until his gift is needed.

Unfortunately, this is not the case. Most people who demonstrate any of the gifts want their gift to shine the brightest. The gifts that were meant to help us get watered down by egos and arrogance.

I can't tell you how many people have walked out of churches because the pastor didn't allow them to share with the church again this week. God forbid someone wants to testify for the thirtieth week in a row and the pastor tells him not this time. I think if one more person stands up with a word of knowledge, telling me I'm going to be blessed, I will throw up. I hope we serve a God that can be more specific than that.

When a church does operate in the gifts with harmony, there is great fellowship. People's lives are truly changed, and the church is healthy.

When we flow in the gifts of the Spirit properly, there is maturity. Maturity is the church walking in balance. Balance causes a church to be healthy.

Think of it this way, how many people want to be around someone who is sick? They are coughing and feverish and look like they just got hit by a truck. Now ask yourself why people don't want to come to church? People don't want to be in a sick church any more than they want to be around someone with the flu.

I wonder what a healthy church really looks like? I wonder what a church that has all the components working together looks like? If we will realize that we have all the gifts in common, and not work against each other, we could get somewhere. But this would take a true shepherd's heart!

WE HAVE COMMON WORSHIP.

The greatest hindrance to fellowship in the church is the lack of compromise in worship. Everybody thinks his way is God's way, but I'm reminded of the lyrics in a song by Newsboys: "He worships while he grooves, she prays and barely moves, but they're both reflecting pure devotion."

We all have a common love for God, but we just express it in different ways. Here's the deal: don't judge what you've not experienced.

I was in Africa teaching at a pastor's conference. When I showed up, the worship was in full swing. People were dancing, shouting, and singing things I had never heard before. One guy was beating on a tin can, another was beating on a piston ring from a car, and another lady was hollering. To my ears, it was the worst noise I had ever heard. There was no tune or tone; there was no rhythm, only noise. But what was present was a desire to please God with their hearts.

I soon joined in with my own dance and my own shout and my own singing. For the first time, they didn't turn my microphone down while I sang. I was not out of place with my dance. We had common ground, and it was called worship.

At Voice to the Nations, we have awesome worship. It's not just the music; it's the heart of the people. They just want to get into the presence of God. At the start of the service (every service), the altars fill up with people desiring to please God with their worship. Moments before the worship begins, you may see people giving each other high fives and embracing. They are getting ready to have common worship. The excitement of getting to experience God flows through the church.

Some will be jumping and dancing, others will be shouting and spinning. We even have those who barely move, maybe only lifting up their hand a time or two. But everybody is responding to worship.

How many times have we missed the opportunity to receive from the Lord because it was not our style of worship? I know that the style of music is important to someone while he is worshiping, but we've gotten so bad in the church that we can only worship to certain songs. I believe God honors the person who can walk in any church and worship no matter what the style. That person will experience true fellowship.

WE HAVE COMMON FELLOWSHIP.

Let's see what the word says about fellowship.

"That which was from the beginning, which we have heard, which we have seen with our eyes, which we have looked at and our hands have touched-this we proclaim concerning the Word of life. The life appeared; we have seen it and testify to it, and we proclaim to you the eternal life, which was with the Father and has appeared to us. We proclaim to you what we have seen and heard, so that you also may have fellowship with us. And our fellowship is with the Father and with his Son, Jesus Christ. We write this to make our joy complete. This is the message we have heard from him and declare to you: God is light; in him there is no darkness at all. If we claim to have fellowship with him yet walk in the darkness, we lie and do not live by the truth. But if we walk in the light, as he is in the light, we have fellowship with one another, and the blood of Jesus, his Son, purifies us from all sin." - 1 John 1:1-7

While looking at 1 John we notice some things. Notice John said that which we have heard, have seen, and have touched. John was speaking of an experience. ***Understanding true fellowship begins with your having an experience with the Lord***. It's hard to relate to others when you've not had an experience yourself. How often have you heard others talking about their experience with God, and all you could do was walk away or doubt what they were saying? If you yourself have an experience, you can relate to the experiences of others.

People too often judge what they don't understand. When you have your own experience, though different, you can relate to the experiences of others. Look again at what verse 3 says, *"We proclaim to you what we have seen and heard, so that you also may have fellowship with us." When I testify of my experience, I'm enabling you to have fellowship with me.* Fellowship goes to the core of our experience. So what is our experience? It's the everyday working of God in our lives.

God is constantly allowing us to have experiences with Him. When He blesses us with a new job, we can testify of it. When He heals our children, we can testify of it. When He turns our situations around for our good, we can testify of it.

Watch what happens in verse 6: *"If we claim to have fellowship with him yet walk in the darkness, we lie and do not live by the truth." When you slip away from God, you lose both fellowship with Him and the church.* When someone walks away from his/her relationship with God, he/she automatically walks away from his/her fellowship with the church.

Ever notice someone who walks away from the church because he decides to do his own thing? He begins to blame and accuse the church, when in reality he is the one who walked away.

We had a couple at our church who fell into sin and left the church. We tried calling them and ministering to them, but they wouldn't answer our calls nor return them. Despite the efforts of myself and my leadership, we simply were unable to connect with this couple.

A couple of months later they ran into one of our members and begin to tell them the church let them down and was not there for them. When you walk away from the church, you allow yourself to step into deception. This is a plan of the enemy, a plan to stop fellowship and hinder you from having a shepherd's heart.

The more someone walks in the light the greater his fellowship will be. Verse 7 says, *"But if we walk in the light, as he is in the light, we have fellowship with one another."* True fellowship comes from those who walk closely with the Lord. You show me someone who has a mature relationship with God, and I'll show you someone who has much fellowship with many people. Often times we complain that we don't have true fellowship among our Christian brothers and sisters. This may be because you don't have true fellowship with God. Think about the hindrances to fellowship: unforgiveness, doubt, fear, and distrust. These are not attributes of a person who is in deep fellowship with the Lord. Fellowship strengthens the shepherd's heart. Why do you think God puts so much importance on fellowship and partnership?

Check out a couple of reasons fellowship is so important.

POWER OF AGREEMENT

"Again, I tell you that if two of you on earth agree about anything you ask for, it will be done for you by my Father in heaven. For where two or three come together in my name, there am I with them." - Matthew 18:19-20

If there is no fellowship in your life, who's going to agree with you? In times of crisis, I don't know about you, but I want someone to stand in the gap with me.

GREATER RETURN ON YOUR LABOR

"There was a man all alone; he had neither son nor brother. There was no end to his toil, yet his eyes were not content with his wealth. 'For whom am I toiling,' he asked, 'and why am I depriving myself of enjoyment?' This too is meaning-less- a miserable business! two are better than one, because they have a good return for their work: If one falls down, his friend can help him up. But pity the man who falls and has no one to help him up! Also, if two lie down together, they will keep warm. But how can one keep warm alone? Though one may be overpowered, two can defend themselves. A cord of three strands is not quickly broken." - Ecclesiastes 4:8-12

A lot of the ineffectiveness of the church is because people are trying do it on their own. The Bible is clear on the fact that two are better than one. No matter how good you think you are, someone else can complement you.

In order for you to have this kind of fellowship, a couple of things have to happen.

First off, you will have to learn to feel something for your brother. We tend to be an emotional people, yet we lack emotion when it comes to other saints in trouble. We judge too quickly when we should be putting ourselves in their shoes.

Next you will need to endure hardship that's not your own. When you start to develop the shepherd's heart, you will find yourself carrying burdens that are not your own. You think they are not your own, but if we are a body then one person's pain does become our pain. We need to realize that when one is affected, then all are affected. There is a never-ending trickle-down effect in the Kingdom of God. One person's shortcomings can become another person's fall. What you overcame, someone else may stumble over.

Lastly, we need to learn to lean. This is hard because this will often require us to swallow our pride and humble ourselves. We need to understand that leaning is trust and trust links us to faith. When I lean on you, I'm learning to lean on the Lord. Leaning has its challenges because you're not just trusting in your own faith, you're trusting in the faith of your brother in Christ. This brings up an important question. Can you be trusted? Can you carry the shepherd's heart? Will you be there for your brother? I hope so, because the next great move of God is depending on you.

7

THE NEXT GREAT MOVE OF GOD

Move of God...

Revival...

Awakening...

Every move of God that takes place in the Church adds to the character of the Church. It's time for us to add the character of love to the body of Christ.

I wished that I could say that the Church is operating in the love that God has called us to operate in; but as I look at the body of Christ, I only see patches of true love for one another.

"A new command I give you: Love one another. As I have loved you, so you must love one another. By this all men will know that you are my disciples, if you love one another."
- John 13:34-35

If we truly loved one another, then shouldn't we be reaching the world at a much faster pace? Shouldn't we be seeing revival breaking out instead of churches breaking up?

I know that we come together in times of crisis. Every church in the city will fill up when tragedy strikes. But tragedy-based revival always seems to fade with the memory of the tragedy.

What if people saw us love one another when there was no need or crisis? What if we covered our fallen ministers instead of calling the media? Not cover up, but cover in love.

I'm so proud of the men's ministry we have here at Voice to the Nations. They are a group of men who have no fear of hugging and loving each other. They share a common love that is amazingly contagious.

I'm astounded every year on our men's retreat. There will be the one guy who is hard as brick. Over the course of the trip, he will see men loving each other unashamedly, and his heart will melt in the hands of a loving God because he has witnessed disciples loving one another. Listen to the words of Peter.

"Now that you have purified yourselves by obeying the truth so that you have sincere love for your brothers, love one another deeply, from the heart." - 1 Peter 1:22

How deep do you love? A move of God will require you to love on a level that runs deeper than the surface of a fake smile. A true characteristic of a disciple is that they love deeply.

FROM THE PULPIT TO THE PEW

Here is where the rubber meets the road. We have been taught our whole lives that it's the pastor's job to love the sheep, after all he is the shepherd. It's time for the shepherds sitting in the pews to rise up and start being there for one another.

When was the last time you looked across the aisle and noticed someone was not there and you began to worry? Let's take it a little further. Did you go beyond wondering? Did you check on them? Or did you forget the moment the service started or the moment you left?

We tend to only check on those we have close partnerships with. As I said earlier in this book, partnership is the key.

Here's the deal, partnership is waiting on you. Be the one who starts a new partnership. Be the one who crosses the invisible barrier of "I don't know you." You may just find yourself opening up a door for not only a new friendship but a move of God as well. The chain reaction can start with you.

IT'S JUST COMMON SENSE

As I write this I am wondering, why am I writing this? It just seems so simple. It seems like it should be common place in the Church, but it's not.

It's not common place to love one another unconditionally. It is common, however, to leave the church the first time your feelings get hurt. It's not common place for the person sitting in the pew to respond to the need of the person sitting next to them. It is common to judge the person sitting next to you based on your so-called maturity level. It's not common place to bare one another's burdens. It is common to think it's the pastor's job to deal with the needs of people.

To participate in the next great move of God, to be a shepherd to your fellow brother or sister in Christ, just use your God-given common sense.

CPSIA information can be obtained at www.ICGtesting.com
Printed in the USA
LVOW062103060412

276439LV00001B/4/P